FATIMA

A Message More Urgent Than Ever

BY LUIZ SÉRGIO SOLIMEO

FATIMA

A Message More Urgent Than Ever

"Jesus wishes to establish devotion to my Immaculate Heart in the world."
— *Our Lady of Fatima, June 13, 1917*

THE AMERICAN SOCIETY FOR THE DEFENSE
OF TRADITION, FAMILY AND PROPERTY—TFP
SPRING GROVE, PENN. 17362

Cover illustration:
The Basilica of Fatima with the International Pilgrim Fatima Virgin statue in the forefront.

Copyright © 2016 The American Society for the Defense of Tradition, Family and Property®—TFP®
1358 Jefferson Road
Spring Grove, Penn. 17362
Tel.: (888) 317-5571
www.TFP.org

First printing 2008
Second printing 2016

The American Society for the Defense of Tradition, Family and Property® and TFP® are registered names of The Foundation for a Christian Civilization, Inc., a 501(c)(3) tax-exempt organization.

ISBN-10: 1-877905-38-0
ISBN-13: 978-1-877-905-38-4
Library of Congress Control Number: 2008920693

Printed in the United States of America.

"Today is the ninetieth
anniversary of the apparitions
of Our Lady of Fatima.
With their powerful call to
conversion and penance, they are
without doubt the most prophetic
of all modern apparitions."

— *Pope Benedict XVI*

*(Regina Cœli Square in front of the Shrine
of Aparecida, Brazil, May 13, 2007)*

❧ CONTENTS ☙

FOREWORD

Robert E. Ritchie
America Needs Fatima, Director

Since its inception in 1985, America Needs Fatima's main objective has been to make Our Lady's Fatima message known and practiced in our beloved country, with special emphasis on prayer, amendment of life and penance.

And based on the Fatima message, the America Needs Fatima ranks have swelled with those who, like the three shepherd children, answered *YES*! when the Blessed Mother asked, "Are you willing to offer yourselves to God and bear all the sufferings He wills to send you, as an act of reparation for the sins by which He is offended, and of supplication for the conversion of sinners?"

Among the many things America Needs Fatima has done to spread Our Lady's message, the distribution of Antonio A. Borelli's *Fatima: Message of Tragedy or Hope?* holds a special place.

This praiseworthy book has already reached a worldwide total of over five million copies—many distributed behind the ex-Iron Curtain, that is, in Eastern Europe and Russia. Tens of thousands of Americans have also read Mr. Borelli's book, which has a deeply analytical character.

In addition to this excellent book, America Needs Fatima members have asked me for an account, written in a narrative style, of the Fatima apparitions. To do this, I asked Mr. Luiz Sérgio Solimeo—a longtime Tradition, Family, and Property member—to write the account based almost entirely on Sister Lucia's memoirs, which contain rich first-hand details from the three shepherds, plus valuable lessons for our spiritual life.

I am confident that you will agree that Mr. Solimeo's book shines by its clarity, and will find its doctrinal aspects and historic facts blended in a pleasant and easy-to-read style. It is my hope it will do an immense good to countless souls.

May Our Lady of the Rosary, who promised the triumph of her Immaculate Heart, bless and protect everyone who reads this account of her Fatima apparitions and message.

PRELIMINARY NOTE

Since this book is destined for widespread distribution, we have sought to make it an easy and pleasant read, despite the grave message that the Virgin of Fatima brought to the world. Thus, we have limited the use of footnotes. While not ignoring the huge bibliography on Fatima, we sought to base ourselves as much as possible on Sister Lucia's memoirs and letters. We have also consulted collections of official documents and some of the best-known works that deal with the Fatima apparitions. That bibliography is presented at the end of the book.

Whenever possible, we chose to use the original Portuguese documents, doing our own English translations even when earlier translations already exist, because of our concern for precision and our desire to maintain the flavor of Sister Lucia's simple and enchanting style.

We have also avoided, as much as possible, to delve into discussions or scholarly comments, doing so only when strictly necessary.

A pilgrim walks on his knees in the rain towards the chapel that marks the place where Our Lady of Fatima appeared.

INTRODUCTION
The Message of Fatima, More Urgent Than Ever

With Sister Lucia having died on February 13, 2005 at the age of 97, some people ask if the last seer's death closes the Fatima cycle, and if Our Lady's message to the three little shepherds is still timely.

To answer these two questions, we must examine from the correct perspective the events and heavenly manifestations that occurred 100 years ago.

Importance of the Messenger and Divine Confirmation

An event of this nature is considered significant based on the importance of the person involved and when its authenticity is proven beyond a doubt. In the case of the Fatima apparitions, the leading person is the most exalted creature of all, the Mother of God; and God Himself authenticated the apparitions by means of the miracle of the sun, an event of biblical proportions.

The Stupendous Miracle of the Sun

Journalist Avelino de Almeida, an atheist, described the events at Cova da Iria in an article titled, "Amazing! How the Sun Danced in Fatima at Noon." What follows is an excerpt of this article published in the Lisbon anticlerical newspaper, *O Século*, on October 15, 1917:

> From beside the parked carriages where many thousands stood, afraid to descend into the muddy soil of the Cova da Iria, we saw the immense crowd turn toward the sun at its highest, free of all clouds. The sun seemed to us like a plate of dull silver. It could be seen without the least effort. It did not blind or burn. It seemed as though an eclipse were taking

place. All of a sudden, a tremendous shout burst forth, "Miracle, miracle!" Before the astonished eyes of the people—whose attitude carried us back to biblical times, and who, white with terror, with heads uncovered, gazed at the sun that trembled and made brusque and unheard of movements beyond all cosmic laws— the sun seemed literally to dance in the sky.

In *Meet the Witnesses*, John Haffert compiled well-documented testimonies from eyewitnesses to the phenomenon. Among these are some who watched it from miles away, such as Father Joaquim Lourenço and writer Afonso Vieira. The existence of these distant witnesses rules out the possibility of mass suggestion.

The Miracle of the Sun took place on October 13, 1917. The light was reflected on the ground; on the trees; and on the very faces of the people. After three mad movements, the globe of fire appeared to tremble, shake and then plunge in a zigzag course toward the multitude.

The Message is Still All-Important

An unprecedented miracle, such as that of the "dancing of the sun," was meant to confirm a likewise unprecedented message from God. Thus, we should look at Fatima as the message of heaven par excellence for our times.

Indeed, the evils this message denounced are ongoing. Likewise, the solution indicated is also still applicable to our days.

What are these evils and the respective solution?

Basically, Mary Most Holy came to remind a world steeped in apostasy of the gravity of sin and its consequences, the punishment of hell for unrepentant sinners, and the chastisement of the world for offending God.

The miracle of the sun was documented by the reporter Avelino de Almeida, from *O Século* of Lisbon in an extensive article published the following Monday, October 15, 1917, and another on the 29th of the same month in *A Ilustração Portuguesa*.

In Fatima, God sent the Queen of Prophets herself

The Fatima apparitions instruct us about the terrible gravity of the world situation and about the true causes of our evils, as well as teach us the means by which we must avoid the earthly and eternal punishments that await us. To people in antiquity, God sent the prophets. In our days, He spoke to us through the Queen of Prophets herself. Having thus studied what Our Lady announced, what can we say?

The only suitable words are those of Our Lord in the Gospel: If any man has ears to hear, let him hear (Mark 4:23).

Plinio Corrêa de Oliveira

To forestall the damnation of so many souls and God's chastisement, Mary Most Holy offered as a solution the devotion to her Immaculate Heart, the Communion of Reparation on the First Saturdays for five consecutive months, and Russia's consecration to her Immaculate Heart.

The Blessed Virgin warned that, if her requests went unheeded, World War II would break out and Communism would spread its errors throughout the world, provoking wars and persecutions of the Church. Finally, she promised divine forgiveness and the triumph of her Immaculate Heart, which would be followed by Russia's consecration and conversion.

It is painfully obvious that her requests were not heeded in time. World War II broke out, and the errors of Russia spread throughout the world, not only with the implementation of Communist regimes in many countries of Europe, Asia and Central America, but equally through the spread of doctrines and customs that are consistently leading the world to abandon natural and Christian order. Drives for homosexual "marriage," abortion and euthanasia are but a few of these manifestations. Therefore, though the power of Communism has somewhat waned in its political form, its cultural aspects are now at their zenith.

In fact, divorce, free love and immodesty find their philosophical systematization and political support in Socialism and Communism, whose driving forces are unbridled sensuality and unrestrained pride. These two vices demolish all barriers and restraints keeping human behavior and thought in accordance with God's law and the order He established.

Thus, we must admit that we are still within a phase of the chastisement foreseen at Fatima and must strive to advance toward that which Our Lady promised: the triumph of her Immaculate Heart.

The message of Fatima is more urgent than ever.

CHAPTER 1

Christian Life in a Portuguese Village

Life in a Portuguese mountain village in the beginning of the 20th century was full of the enchantment, peace and tranquility that result from one's sense of duty and the consolations of the Faith.

A Hardworking Life, Filled With Faith

It was a hardworking life marked by tilling fields, shepherding and domestic chores, paced with prayers along the day and liturgical feasts throughout the year. Work and prayer mixed naturally, as well as the simple entertainment of engaging in animated conversations or chanting nostalgic or joyful songs accompanied by a guitar, fifes and flutes.

That simple life, very no-nonsense and down to earth, but with one's eyes set on heaven, maintained families united and created profound and lasting bonds of friendship among neighbors.

The village was like a large family where everyone knew one another, helped one another, depended on one another, shared one another's works, joys and sadness, supported one another in sickness and in need, and consoled one another in misfortune, practicing Christian charity.

Aljustrel, on the slopes of the Serra do Aire, was a hamlet belonging to the parish of the village of Fatima, about 80 miles north of Portugal's capital, Lisbon, and 53 miles south of Coimbra, the former capital of the first Portuguese kings and home to its celebrated university.

It is there that our story begins.

Two Families Intertwine

The Santos and Ferreira da Rosa families were the most prosperous in Aljustrel, owning some rural properties and houses, but working as hard as anyone else nonetheless.

Profoundly religious, the families were bound by two marriages: Antonio dos Santos married Maria Rosa; and Antonio's sister, Olimpia, married José, Maria Rosa's brother.

Antonio and Maria Rosa had six daughters and a son; the youngest of all, Lucia, born on March 22, 1907, would become the main Fatima seer along with her cousins Francisco and Jacinta.

Lucia with her family after the death of her father in 1920.

The Marto family poses on the stairs of a neighboring home.

These were Olimpia's children, who after losing her husband José, had married Manuel Pedro Marto, her distant relative, with whom she had seven children, the youngest of whom were Francisco, born on June 11, 1908, and Jacinta, born on March 11, 1910.

Intensity of Family Life

In reading Sister Lucia's memoirs, one senses with nostalgia the intense Christian family life of her childhood:

The sun had barely risen when work started in the fields, caring for animals, egg-laying hens and chickens raised for food. Everyone had his or her own specific tasks, something which, far from being regarded as a burden, was seen as a perfect way for all in the family to be on the same page.

In fact, it was amidst the constant occupations that family members related with one another and with neighbors. Rural life was a common denominator of the mountain village's inhabitants.

Occupations seemed natural to those simple people who saw their laborious life as the Lord's blessing, an honest and religious way to make a living in the joy of fulfilling one's duty and accepting one's own lot, and the toils were an occasion for conversations, chants and prayers. Especially at night, as the family gathered, while the sisters knitted or sewed, a brother would play the guitar and everyone would sing, drawing neighbors to come in to partake in that joy, commenting in laughter, "Since you won't let us go to sleep, we've come to join the singing."

In those evening sessions, they would also entertain themselves telling old stories passed on down through generations, legends of enchanted castles or fabulous battles. The mother, however, would not miss those occasions to tell episodes of sacred history or the lives of the saints.

Maria Rosa was one of the few women in the village who knew how to read, having been taught by an aunt, a pious lady who taught young girls out of charity. From that pious aunt Maria Rosa had also inherited some books that she liked to read on Sundays—she said she would rather converse with saints than with her female neighbors. During the week, at the noon break, she would teach Christian Doctrine to her youngest daughters.

Christian Charity

The charity of Lucia's family was proverbial. When they baked bread in the oven or crushed olives to extract their delicious oil, they would always reserve some for the poor. The poor would often come begging for alms and, when not from the area, also to be put up for the evening. Once, when Antonio gave alms to a poor man who knocked on the door, Antonio asked prayers for himself and for Lucia, who stood next to him. Maria Rosa protested in good humor, "So you asked no prayers for me?" Antonio answered with a smile, "What is mine is yours, and therefore praying for me is the same as praying for you." Maria Rosa agreed, satisfied.

When someone was sick in the village they would come ask Lucia's mother for help; she would care for the sick out of charity. When Maria Rosa was busy, she would send a daughter in her place.

Once Lucia, already 11 years old, was sent to stay with a poor widow's sick son, thereby allowing the widow time to get some rest. The young man was at the last stage of tuberculosis and spent the whole time sitting in bed so he could breathe. Lucia would often fan him so he could breathe better, and he would thank her, smiling and saying, "It seems that time goes by quicker when you're here."

Someone warned her father that it was imprudent to have her stay with a patient with tuberculosis because of the risk of contagion. The father answered with simplicity, "God will not repay me with evil the good I do for Him." Sister Lucia, who wrote about this episode when she was 82, commented that so far she had never fallen ill with that sickness.

A Wholesome and Realistic Education

Lucia's mother, a good teacher, had not only a sense of reality of things natural but also supernatural, and she would not hesitate to speak to the children about hell, instilling in them a healthy fear of offending God.

Thus it was that once, one of the children whom her mother out of charity would let stay with her daughters while their mothers tilled the fields, said a bad word. Maria Rosa, sweetly but firmly, reprehended the child saying that it was a sin, that it displeased the Child Jesus and that those who sinned would go to hell. Those words made a healthy impression on the little Jacinta, who was present.

Chaste Courtship for a Happy Marriage

One of Lucia's sisters, already at an adult age, commented with her parents that a young man had proposed that they keep company, looking to get married, but she was doubtful because another man had proposed first. Her mother answered that what mattered was for the suitor to be serious and chaste, for her to flee those who proposed bad things, because it is better to stay single than to make a bad marriage. And her father added,

> When I proposed to court your mother, the first thing we agreed on was to keep pure the flower of our chastity until our marriage to offer it to God in exchange for his blessing and the children He might be willing to give us. Thus He has blessed us with this little crowd.

Lucia's First Holy Communion

Prayer was an integral part of family life. Lucia learned to say the Hail Mary while still in her mother's arms. As she was intelligent and had a good memory, Lucia learned the catechism from listening to her mother teach it to her siblings and neighbors. When Carolina, her older sister, began to attend catechism class at the parish church in preparation for her First Holy Communion, Maria Rosa sent Lucia along despite being only six years of age.

When the time came to set a date for the ceremony, the pastor informed the six year old that she could not receive Communion with the others. Upon hearing this, Lucia cried her heart out, leaning imploringly on the good pastor's knees. At that precise moment, Father Cruz, an exemplary priest and tireless missionary, walked in and asked the reason for her tears.

Upon hearing the cause, he called Lucia aside and questioned her in detail. "Father Pena," he said to the pastor after questioning Lucia, "you can allow this girl to receive. She knows what she is doing better than many of these older ones." The pastor demurred because of her age, but the famous priest replied, "It doesn't matter. I will take the responsibility." And thus Lucia was allowed to receive her First Communion at the age of six.

Mystical Grace

The happy Lucia told her mother all about it and asked to make her first confession to Father Cruz, which she did. But on leaving the confessional she realized that everyone else in line for confession was laughing.

Her mother then explained that, in confession, one must whisper. She had spoken so loudly that everyone had heard her sins. Still, no one heard the priest's advice to her. Sister Lucia tells us herself in her memoirs, "My daughter," said the missionary, "your soul is the temple of the Holy Ghost. Keep it always pure so that He may continue His divine action upon it."

"At these words," writes Sister Lucia, "I was filled with respect for my soul, and I asked my good confessor how I should do this." "Go before the altar of Our Lady, and, on your knees, trustingly ask her to take your heart, and prepare it to receive her dear Son tomorrow in a worthy manner. Ask that He may keep your heart for Himself alone."

Sister Lucia continues,

> There was more than one statue of Our Lady in the church. But as my sisters were in charge of adorning the altar of Our Lady of the Rosary, I had the habit of praying before that statue, and that is where I knelt again. I asked her with all the fervor of which my heart was capable, to keep my heart for God alone.

On repeating this humble prayer with my eyes fixed
on the statue, it seemed to me she smiled, and looking
at me kindly was telling me, "Yes." I was filled with
so much joy that I could hardly speak.

On the next day, as a last recommendation, Maria Rosa told
Lucia to ask Our Lord to make her, Lucia, a saint. Lucia writes
of this memorable moment,

When the priest came down the altar steps, my
heart beat so hard that it felt as if it was leaping from
my chest. But as soon as the divine Host touched my
tongue, complete serenity and peace came over me. I
felt penetrated by a supernatural atmosphere in
which God's presence was so sensible that I seemed
to see and hear Him. It was then I asked Him: "Lord,
make me a saint, keep my heart always pure, and for
You alone."

Lucia added,

Here it seemed to me that our good God said to me
in the depths of my heart these clear words, "The
grace granted to you today will always be alive in
your soul, producing fruits of eternal life." I felt so
transformed in God! . . . From that day on I lost the
attraction I was beginning to feel for the things of the
world and would only be comfortable in a solitary
place where, alone, I could recall the delights of my
First Communion.

CHAPTER 2
Three Little Shepherds

Francisco's and Jacinta's family life was no different than Lucia's in piety and hard work. Their father, "Uncle Marto," as he was known to everyone, though illiterate, was intelligent and a good observer. He had been to Africa as a soldier and fought in the wars against the rebels during 1895–1896 in Mozambique, a Portuguese colony at the time.

According to testimony collected by Canon Dr. Formigão at the time of the Fatima events, Mr. Marto was considered the "most serious man of the place, incapable of deceiving anyone whatsoever."

Father John de Marchi, I.M.C., author of important books on Fatima, where he lived for a while, was surprised at Mr. Marto's extensive knowledge of Catholic doctrine, as well as his good sense, uprightness, selflessness and courage.

Writing about the way her little cousins used to be before the apparitions, Sister Lucia recognizes that Jacinta was a bit spoiled and that Francisco, who was excessively peaceful, had a tendency not to care about anything. But they were very innocent and generous children.

The three cousins were inseparable and used to play in the

Left: **Ti Marto, the father of Jacinta and Francisco Marto.**
Right: **One of the paths used by the three children.**

Lucia dos Santos, Francisco and Jacinta Marto, the three shepherd children to whom Our Lady of Fatima appeared.

courtyard of Lucia's home next to a well surrounded by trees. Jacinta also liked to watch the sunset with her cousins and then gaze at the sky counting the stars. The children called the stars "Angels' candles," the sun "Our Lord's candle," and the moon "Our Lady's candle." The little one used to say that she preferred "Our Lady's candle" because it was not as hard on the eyes as "Our Lord's candle."

When Lucia turned seven she replaced her sister Carolina, who had turned thirteen, in taking care of the sheep. The two little cousins, who liked to play only with her, were disconsolate but would come to see her at the end of the day as soon as they heard the sheep's little bells ringing.

Apparitions of the Angel

With her lively and intelligent imagination and fearlessness, Lucia had a gift to attract and lead other children. As soon as they heard she would shepherd her family's sheep, all the little shepherds from the region wanted to go with her, so a large group of children would go together to the pastures on the mountain range.

In 1915, the first of the many extraordinary phenomena that would mark Lucia's life took place. She narrates,

> More or less around noon we ate our lunch and then I invited my companions to say a Rosary with me, to which they gladly agreed. Barely had we started when we saw before our eyes, as if suspended in the air upon the trees, a figure like a statue of snow which the rays of the sun turned into something transparent.
>
> "What's that?" asked my girlfriends, kind of scared.
> "I don't know!"
>
> We continued our prayer with our eyes always set on the figure, which disappeared as soon as we finished.

Lucia said nothing at home, but the other children did tell

their own families so Lucia's mother got word of it and asked her about it. Not knowing how to explain herself, she said it looked like a person "wrapped in a bedsheet," to which her mother answered firmly, "Childish foolishness!"

That mysterious episode, which seems to have been a remote preparation for the future events, was repeated twice. Lucia's mother was upset with her, and her sisters started mocking her. She was thus beginning to taste the suffering that would embitter her life in the future—the animosity of her family, which up until then had treated her only with utmost tenderness.

The following year, 1916, Francisco and Jacinta were allowed by their parents to take their family's herds along with those of Lucia's. The inseparable trio was back together.

One "beautiful day," as Lucia puts it in her simple language, the three cousins, after shepherding for a while, went up the Cabeço hill to eat their lunch and say the Rosary. A fine rain was falling and they entered a grotto for cover. They stayed a long time in it even though the rain had stopped and the sun had come out.

Lucia narrates what happened next:

A representation of the third apparition of the Angel of Portugal to Lucia, Jacinta and Francisco during the summer of 1916.

Courtesy of Felipe Barandiaran

We ate our lunch, said our Rosary and I don't know whether it was one of those hasty ones in which, dying to go out and play, we would simply run through our beads saying only the words Hail Mary and Our Father! Once our prayer was finished, we began to play throwing little stones.

We had been playing for a few moments when a strong wind shook the trees and made us raise our eyes to see what was going on, since it was a calm day. We then saw that above the olive trees the figure I've already spoken about was walking toward us. Jacinta and Francisco had never seen it, nor had I ever spoken to them about it. As it drew nearer, we could make out its traits: It was a young man 14 or 15 years old, whiter than snow whom the sun made as transparent as crystal, and of a great beauty. When he got near us he said, "Fear not! I am the Angel of Peace. Pray with me."

And kneeling down, he bowed his head all the way to the ground and made us repeat three times these words, "My God! I believe, I adore, I hope and I love Thee. I ask Thee forgiveness for those who do not believe, do not adore, do not hope and do not love Thee."

Then, rising, he said, "Pray like this. The Hearts of Jesus and Mary are attentive to the voice of your supplications."

His words were so engraved in our minds that we would never forget them. And after that we spent a long time prostrated, repeating them until we got tired. I soon recommended that we should keep it a secret and this time, thanks be to God, they did as I asked.

This first apparition of the Angel to the three shepherds

together was also the first time when the Angel allowed the children to see him clearly in the shape of an adolescent and began to prepare them for their future mission. That was a milestone in their lives, a departure from the innocent but ordinary life of the peasants in a very Catholic region and the beginning of an extraordinary life of heroism.

Some time later, the children were playing near the well in Lucia's home when the Angel appeared for the second time:

"What are you doing? Pray, pray a lot. The Sacred Hearts of Jesus and Mary have designs of mercy upon you. Constantly offer prayers and sacrifices to the Most High."

"How must we sacrifice?" [Lucia] asked.

"In all that you can, offer God a sacrifice in reparation for the sins with which He is offended and in supplication for the conversion of sinners. You will thus attract peace upon your country. I am the guardian Angel of Portugal. Above all, accept and bear with submission the suffering that the Lord sends you."

Courtesy of Felipe Barandiaran

The well at Lucia's house where the Angel appeared to the young shepherds for the second time.

At this second apparition the Angel continued to attract the children to a more perfect life of acceptance and conformity with God's will.

The third and last apparition of the Angel, in Lucia's words, took place as follows:

A long time elapsed and we went to shepherd our herds on a property of my parents located on the slope of the said hill, a little above Valinhos. It is an olive grove that we called Pregueira. Having had our lunch, we agreed to go pray at the grotto on the slope of [Cabeço]. So we went around the slope and had to climb up a few rocks on top of Pregueira. The sheep managed to pass with great difficulty.

As soon as we got there we started to repeat the Angel's prayer on our knees and with our faces to the ground, "My God! I believe, I adore, I hope and love Thee, etc. I don't know how many times we had repeated this prayer, when we saw an unknown light shining upon us. We arose to see what was happening and saw the Angel, holding in his left hand a Chalice over which was suspended a Host from which a few drops of blood were dripping into the Chalice. The Angel left the Chalice suspended in the air, knelt next to us and made us repeat three times:

"Most Holy Trinity, Father, Son, Holy Spirit, I adore Thee profoundly and offer Thee the most precious Body, Blood, Soul and Divinity of Jesus Christ present in all the tabernacles on earth in reparation for the insults, sacrileges and indifference with which He is offended. And through the infinite merits of His Most Sacred Heart and the Immaculate Heart of Mary, I ask Thee for the conversion of poor sinners."

He then stood up and took the Chalice and the Host

in his hands. He gave me the Sacred Host and distributed the Blood in the Chalice between Jacinta and
Francisco, saying at the same time, "Eat and drink the
Body and Blood of Jesus Christ, horribly insulted by
ungrateful men. Make reparation for their crimes and
console your God."

And prostrating himself again on the ground, he
repeated the same prayer with us another three times:
"Most Holy Trinity . . . etc." and disappeared. We
remained in that posture, always repeating the same
words; and when we arose we saw that it was night,
time for us to go home.

Despite the goodness the Angel manifested, his superior
nature left the poor children as if annihilated. For a long time
after the visions they were unable to speak or move. Even a
few days later they would feel some difficulty doing so.

Already present in those first supernatural manifestations
was something that would become a mysterious constant:
Lucia alone would take the initiative and speak, Jacinta would
only see and hear, while Francisco would only see but be
unable to hear anything.

While these events were taking place, others modified the
village's life and Lucia's family. The parish priest, Father Pena,
was replaced by a more severe pastor, Father Manuel Marques
Ferreira, known by a nickname, as was common in Portuguese
villages at the time, as Father Boicinha. He combated the peasants' excessive love of dancing and that custom gradually disappeared among the adults and children.

Lucia's father fell into bad company, abusing wine and
neglecting his business, so the family lost several properties.
Two of the seer's sisters married and left home; Lucia's mother, because of the economic setbacks, sent two of her other
daughters to work as housemaids (they returned after a while,

when Lucia's mother fell ill).

Lucia understood even better what suffering was when she saw her mother, at supper time, look at the empty places around the table, bend her head down and cry, "My God! Where has the joy of this home gone?!"

CHAPTER 3

"Fear Not—I Am from Heaven"

In that tranquil mountain region of Portugal, May 13, 1917, "dawned as beautiful and as smiling as many other days," Lucia recounts. It was spring, the Sunday prior to the Ascension. The three little shepherds went to Mass at the neighboring chapel of Boleiros (offered for the poor souls of Purgatory) and from there they took their sheep grazing.

Despite the Angel's earlier apparitions, the three children were far from assuming that something extraordinary was about to happen. They had taken the sheep to one of the family's properties, the Cova da Iria, and, as Lucia narrates, were playing totally relaxed and unconcerned. On that occasion, Lucia was ten years old, Francisco was nine and Jacinta was only seven.

But let Sister Lucia recall what happened:

> Having gone to play with Jacinta and Francisco, on top of the slope at Cova da Iria, building a little wall around a bush, we suddenly saw, as it were, a flash of lightning.
>
> "We'd better go home," I said to my cousins, "as thunder may follow lightning."
>
> "All right."
>
> And we started descending the slope, herding the sheep toward the road. As we got more or less to the middle of the slope, near a large *azinheira*[1] [holm oak] that stood there, we saw another flash of lightning and a few steps further we saw upon the tree a Lady all dressed in white, more brilliant than the Sun, spreading a light clearer and more intense than a crys-

---

1. Speaking about the holm oak, Lucia sometimes refers to a *carrasqueira*, other times to an *azinheira*. She explained to Father McGlyn that "a young *azinheira* at that age is called a *carrasqueira*."

tal glass full of crystalline water crossed by the rays of the most ardent sun. We stopped, surprised by the apparition. We were so close that we stood inside the light that surrounded Her or that She spread, about a meter and a half away.

Then Our Lady told us, "Don't be afraid. I will not hurt you."

"Where are You from?" I asked.

"I am from heaven."

"And what do You want from me?"

"I came to ask you to come here six months in a row on the thirteenth at this same time. Later I will tell you who I am and what I want. Then I will return here a seventh time."

Lucia dos Santos, 10, was the oldest of the three seers.

"And will I also go to heaven?"

"Yes, you will."

"And Jacinta?"

"Also."

"And Francisco?"

"Also, but he has to pray many Rosaries."

Then I remembered to ask about two young ladies who had recently died. They were my friends and were staying in my house so my older sister would teach them how to weave.

"Is Maria das Neves already in heaven?"

"Yes, she is."

It seems to me she was about 16 years old.

"And what about Amelia?"

"She will be in Purgatory until the end of the world."[2]

I think she was about 18 or 20 years old.

"Do you wish to offer yourselves to God to bear all the sufferings that He may wish to send you, in reparation for the sins with which He is offended and in supplication for the conversion of sinners?"

"Yes, we do."

"Go, then, for you will have much to suffer, but the grace of God will be your comfort."

It was on pronouncing these last words that She opened her hands for the first time, communicating to us a light so intense, like reflections from her hands, that penetrated our chests and the innermost part of our souls, making us see ourselves in God. God was this light, making us see ourselves more clearly than we see ourselves in the best of mirrors. Then, through an intimate impulse also communicated to us, we fell on our knees and repeated in our minds, "O Most Holy Trinity, I adore Thee. My God, my God, I love Thee in the Blessed Sacrament."

The first few moments having passed, Our Lady added, "Pray the Rosary every day to obtain peace for the world and the end of the [First World] War."

She then began to rise serenely, ascending toward the east until she disappeared in the immense distance. The light that surrounded her, as it were, gradually opened a way amid the stars, and this is why sometimes we said we had seen heaven opening up.

With the generosity proper of their innocence, the three chil-

---

2. Father Sebastião Martins dos Reis, who researched about Amelia, informs us that she died in circumstances involving dishonor in matters of chastity. When Father McGlynn, O.P., interviewing Sister Lucia, showed surprise at the word by Our Lady that the girl would be in Purgatory to the end of the world, the Fatima seer recalled that others go to hell for all eternity because of a single mortal sin, something incomparably more tragic than staying in Purgatory until the end of the world.

dren had accepted the request, "Do you want to suffer to make reparation for sins and to convert sinners?" And the suffering would not be long in coming.

Lucia, quite mature for her years, asked and even begged her cousins, particularly Jacinta, not to tell anything to anyone. She had an intuition that if that happened, hurricanes of incomprehension would be unleashed upon them.

In spite of her solemn promise, the little Jacinta, beside herself with joy, could not help but tell her mother everything as soon as she saw her.

Without having believed her, Olimpia Marto, finding it a picturesque childish invention, asked her to repeat the story over dinner to the whole family. Her brothers laughed and mocked, but the prudent Mr. Marto kept silent. If Our Lady had appeared other times, why could she not have done so now? Above all,

---

"There Are no Words to Express Her Beauty"

Here is Sister Lucia's description of the apparition to the sculptor, Father Thomas McGlynn, O.P., as she answered his questions:

"She was surrounded by light and was in the middle of light. Her feet rested on the *azinheira*. She always had a star on her tunic . . . [and] a cord with a little ball of light [around her neck]. I never saw her hair. The mantle was made of light and so was her tunic: there were two waves of light, one on top of the other."

"How old did Our Lady appear to be?"

"Perhaps seventeen."

"Did the face and hands and feet of Our Lady

have the color of light or the color of flesh?"

"Flesh-colored light, light which took on the color of flesh."

"Did the apparition strain your eyes?"

"It didn't really hurt my eyes but was a very intense light and we felt some difference. Our eyesight was not powerful enough."

"Was the yellow light all around the bottom of the mantle?"

"It is my impression that it was all around. The intensity of this light seemed to be a reflection of the light from within."

"Was she always sad?"

"She never smiled. She was pleasant, but sad."

"What do you say of her beauty?"

"There are no words to express her beauty."

his daughter had never lied in her life and Francisco, who confirmed her report, was very calm and collected.

The reaction of Lucia's mother was altogether different. Hearing about the episode from her daughter, Maria dos Anjos, she immediately showed complete opposition. On top of all the setbacks the family had suffered recently, all she needed was for her youngest daughter to come up with such stories in so grave a matter! Who was that girl for Our Lady to deign to appear to her?

Unable to make her daughter recant, she took her to the parish priest, Father Manuel Marques Ferreira, so he would find a way to oblige Lucia to say she had lied.

The pastor acted with prudence. He questioned the girl and recommended that her mother follow the case carefully and not forbid Lucia to go to the place of the apparitions on the set dates.

The pastor's annotations about his conversation with the seer reproduce faithfully Lucia's dialogue with Our Lady. It is the first document about the apparitions and confirms that she never varied in her narrations. Later, the pastor proceeded to question the three seers after each apparition.

That May 13 would not only change the lives of three innocent children but become a milestone of a renewed devotion to Our Lady throughout the world, serve as an occasion for innumerable conversions, and give rise to theological, cultural and even political reflections and disputes.

One thing is for sure. The Fatima events that began on that tranquil spring Sunday leave no one indifferent—people either take the Blessed Mother's words seriously or combat them by every means.

As poet Paul Claudel put it, the Fatima events appear "as an explosion, a violent eruption, I would even dare say scandalous, of the supernatural world inside the borders of this agitated and materialistic earthly world."

CHAPTER 4

The Immaculate Heart: The Way That Leads to God

The change in Francisco and Jacinta was so extraordinary that despite their short lifetimes they can be compared to the great penitent saints.

If penance is heroic in adults, in children, who are much more delicate, it goes beyond the limits of mere human nature and shows the power of supernatural action in a more stupendous fashion. Furthermore, since they were innocent children, their acts of penance were a fruit of complete selflessness and intense charity toward poor sinners.

This is where the Communion of Saints' dogma attains all its significance: God accepts the sacrifices and prayers of generous souls to placate his justice and to grant special graces to certain sinners or maintain hesitating souls in virtue.

Since the main source about the Fatima events is Sister Lucia, she naturally emphasizes in her narrations the heroic acts of penance of her cousins but remains very discreet about her own. However, she not only associated herself with those acts, but also bore a very painful moral suffering, which her cousins were spared—scorn from her family and especially, incomprehension from her mother.

Until then, as the youngest daughter with a joyful temperament and above-average intelligence, she had been treated with all tenderness by her par-

Jacinta Marto, 7, was the youngest of the three seers.

ents and her brothers and sisters.

Divine Providence permitted Lucia's mother, a woman of lively faith and ardent charity, to form the certainty that her daughter was lying. She adamantly held to this opinion during the whole period of the apparitions, became hesitant after the miracle of the sun, but changed entirely only later, when church authorities recognized the veracity of the apparitions.

Although joyful and uninhibited, Lucia was very affectionate and suffered intensely when her family withdrew their tender treatment. And such sufferings in childhood, given the emotional stage proper to that age, are usually more intense and harder to bear than in adulthood.

Her mother's incredulity and the consequent hostility of her siblings, in spite of the suffering it caused, ended by favoring the credibility of the apparitions. In fact, Lucia's family was not only against the apparitions but did everything to dissuade her from continuing to believe in them. Lucia's unshakable constancy amidst that hostility was a sign that what she was saying was authentic.

How can it be explained, from the psychological standpoint, that a girl like Lucia, known to be pious and obedient, would find strength not only to disobey but to contradict the strong personality of her mother, who was, so to speak, the counselor of the village to whom everyone went to solve their personal problems? How can one not see here the intervention of a force superior to the child's capacity, supporting her?

As for Jacinta and Francisco, their parents did not take a hostile attitude toward the apparitions as did Lucia's. Furthermore, Mr. Marto's fame as the most honest and truthful man in town, and his uprightness and selflessness, prevented the least suspicion from being raised against them.

As always happens in such cases, the news that Our Lady had appeared to the three little shepherds spread throughout the region. Accordingly, most people treated the whole thing as a joke, making wisecracks and mocking the children.

When they passed on the roads taking their herds to pasture, neighbors and curious bystanders would make comments, laugh and shake their heads. The poor children were humiliated but bore everything with patience, remembering the Angel's words, "In all that you can, offer God a sacrifice as an act of reparation for the sins with which He is offended and in supplication for the conversion of sinners." The children were also mindful of the Blessed Mother's request, "Do you want to offer yourselves to God to bear all the sufferings He wishes to send you, in reparation for the sins with which He is offended and in supplication for the conversion of sinners?" To which they had answered courageously, "We do."

But there is always a more balanced minority of people who do not rule out a possibility without having sufficient reasons to do so; and on the other hand, there are others who feel an innate attraction to the marvelous and are open to extraordinary manifestations; and a very large number of others are dragged invincibly by curiosity.

June 13, the date set for the Virgin's second apparition, was, and continues to be, a great feast day for the Portuguese. It is the celebration of the great Saint Anthony (1195–1231). Due to the fact that he was born in Lisbon and died in Padua, Italy, the Portuguese call him "Saint Anthony of Lisbon" while the Italians, and almost everyone around the world, call him "Saint Anthony of Padua."

Thus, in villages and cities on the days preceding the feast everyone was preparing for the great day by planning a liturgical feast with solemn Mass, a procession, and a popular feast with fairs, shows and entertainment. At the Fatima parish, the feast was especially celebrated because the glorious Portuguese saint was its patron.

Many people, even the families of the three little shepherds, were certain that they, particularly Jacinta, would never miss the feast of Saint Anthony because of a childish illusion. For the same reason, no one would show up at Cova da Iria, and if the shepherds insisted on being there they would find themselves all alone.

Jacinta's and Francisco's parents, as well as Lucia's, avoided going to the place of the apparitions. It was a prudential measure on their part, to make clear they were not influencing the children.

Contrary to expectations, not only were the three cousins there but about fifty people were also present, presaging the great crowds to come, having skipped the festivities of Saint Anthony in the hope of being with the Queen of Saints, Mary Most Holy.

One of the persons present, Maria Carreira, would play an important role in the Fatima history in her effort to build a chapel at Cova da Iria, a fact that gained her the sobriquet "Maria da Capelinha" ("Mary of the Little Chapel"). Of an ardent and resolute temperament, this peasant woman, filled with faith, would not pass up the chance to see an extraordinary event. To her incredulous husband, who wanted her not to show up at the place of the announced apparition, she argued that no one would fail to stand by the roadside if he knew the king or queen would be passing by (the monarchy had only recently been abolished). "Now then, if they say Our Lady will appear at Cova da Iria, I will not be the one to miss it." Only one of her sons, an invalid, accepted her invitation to come along. The others went to the festivities of Saint Anthony.

Sister Lucia will now describe, with her usual simplicity, the new apparition:

June 13, 1917. After saying the Rosary with Jacinta and Francisco and other persons present, we

again saw the reflection of light drawing near, which
we called lightning, and then Our Lady over the holm
oak, [just as it happened] in May.

"What do you want of me?" I asked.

"I want you to come here on the thirteenth of next
month, pray the Rosary every day, and then that you
learn to read. Later I will say what I want."

I asked for the cure of a sick person.

"If he converts he will be cured during the year."

"I wanted to ask you to take us to heaven."

"Yes, I will take Jacinta and Francisco soon. But
you will stay some more time. Jesus wants to use you
to make me known and loved. He wants to establish
devotion to my Immaculate Heart in the world. To
those who accept it, I promise salvation and those
souls will be loved by God as flowers I have placed
to embellish His Throne."

"Do I stay here alone?" I asked with sorrow.

"No daughter. Do you suffer a lot? Don't be discouraged. I will never leave you. My Immaculate
Heart will be your refuge and the way that will lead
you to God."

The moment she said those words she opened her
hands and communicated to us for the second time the
reflection of that immense light. In it we saw ourselves, as it were, submerged in God. Jacinta and
Francisco appeared to be in the part of the light that
rose to heaven, while I was in the one spreading upon
the earth. In front of the palm of Our Lady's right
hand was a heart surrounded with thorns that
appeared to be piercing it. We understood it was the
Immaculate Heart of Mary, insulted by the sins of
humanity, which wanted reparation.

Also this time Our Lady did not ask us to keep it a secret, but we felt God was moving us to do so.

Our Lady's words at Cova da Iria were the great message of that glorious Saint Anthony's day, "[Jesus] wants to establish devotion to my Immaculate Heart in the world." That Immaculate Heart will be the "refuge" of pious souls and a safe path to salvation, the way that leads to God.

The whole theology of devotion to Our Lady and to her Immaculate Heart is summarized right there: It is Jesus who wants to establish His Mother's triumph; it is He Who has established her as the way that leads to God. The divine will being the expression of God's wisdom, it is according to His

---

The Early Believers

Mrs. Leopoldina Reis told Father De Marchi,

About fourteen of us who had made our first Communion with Lucia joined together and decided to go with her to Cova da Iria. As usual, when Lucia proposed something, no one disagreed.

We were in a group, all ready to go, when Lucia's brother, Antonio, came up to us and said, "Don't go to the Cova, Lucia. If you promise not to, I'll give you some money." And Lucia looked back at him and said, "Money? I don't care about money. What I want is to see the Lady." And we went on for about 300 feet, with Antonio still trying to stop us. He did not succeed, and while we continued on, I noticed Lucia becoming more serious and thoughtful all the while.

Maria da Capelinha, who went to Cova da Iria accompanied by her invalid son, also told Father De Marchi,

Then more people came and at last about 11

o'clock, the children to whom Our Lady had appeared, with some little friends and people from quite far away. . . . Then a girl from Boleiros began to read aloud from a book of prayers which she had brought. . . . Just as the girl from Boleiros was beginning the Litany, Lucia interrupted suddenly, explaining there would not be time to continue. She stood up now and called out to Jacinta, "Don't you see the lightning? Our Lady must be coming!" The three children ran for the holm oak tree, while the rest of us hurried after them, and knelt down on the stony ground. I watched Lucia raise her hands, as though in prayer. We heard her speak to someone who, if there at all, was not visible. There was only one mysterious effect to support our impression of another presence there. We heard something buzzing like a small voice, but could not understand what it was trying to say.

plans that we go to Him through Mary Most Holy.

As Saint Louis Grignon de Montfort says, God, who wanted the participation of Mary in the Incarnation, also wanted to unite her with the work of Redemption. She is so bound together with her Son as to have become the "door" through which we reach Him, the *Janua Coeli,* Gate of Heaven, as we invoke her in her litany.

In a few words to the humble little shepherds, Our Lady summarized volumes on Marian theology.

CHAPTER 5

The Saving Message

After the consolation of having seen Our Lady a second time, the three little shepherds went through a great trial: The pastor, while questioning the three children in the presence of Lucia's mother, raised the hypothesis that the apparitions might be a trick of the devil. This was not a far-fetched supposition, for Saint Paul warns us, "Satan himself transformeth himself into an angel of light" to deceive men (2 Corinthians 11:14).

The Church recommends extreme prudence regarding supernatural manifestations. Two extreme positions should be avoided: On the one hand, an a priori refusal of the supernatural, as if God could not manifest Himself; on the other hand, an excessive credulity that accepts any statement about visions and revelations without a prudent and accurate examination. Above all, in this matter one should give one's definitive acceptance only after the Church has made a pronouncement about it.

Fatima's good pastor could not fail to consider the hypothesis of an intervention by the Evil One, but prudence would require that he not manifest that hypothesis unless he had concrete indications. However, be it by insecurity, because of the enormous responsibility he faced, or by the tension caused by such uncommon events, he ended by doing so before the very eyes of the seers and Lucia's mother. Facing that terrifying possibility, Lucia's mother had her certainties reinforced regarding the falsity of the apparitions and her anguish grew even more. Additionally, in view of the pastor's words, Lucia herself was shaken and began to doubt her own feelings about the Lady who appeared to them. What if she was the devil in disguise?

What an atrocious suffering! On the one hand, Lucia felt an

irresistible attraction for the goodness, beauty, seriousness and candor of the Lady; her words so full of wisdom, her deeply touching requests. On the other hand, a cruel thought: Was she not being deceived by the Evil Angel?

So Lucia told Jacinta and Francisco that she would no longer go to Cova da Iria, and that on the next July 13 they should go on their own. Her cousins were sad and disconcerted. Would that not be a sin, to disobey the Lady who had commanded them to go there? Then, Lucia was the one who spoke with Her, so how could they go by themselves? As far as they were concerned, they had not the least doubt that it was the Most Holy Virgin who appeared. The fervor that possessed them, the wholesome action of the apparition on their souls, was sufficient proof to them of the phenomenon's divine origin. Furthermore, Jacinta argued with her youthful logic, did the Lady not say she was from heaven?

But Lucia was profoundly disturbed and would not be moved by the arguments and appeals of her cousins. She said emphatically, "I will never return to Cova da Iria." It all appeared to be over. Jacinta and Francisco went into a profound affliction and started to pray intensely.

On the eve of the appointed date, Lucia went to sleep totally decided to stand by her word to close the chapter of the apparitions. Nevertheless, when July 13 dawned she felt an unknown force that made her get dressed in a hurry and run to her cousins' house. Jacinta and Francisco were kneeling down next to a bed, praying. "Let's go quick," Lucia said simply, and the two cousins, exulting with joy, left with her to keep the appointment with the Lady.

A small crowd of about five thousand people was already gathered at the place of the apparitions. A majority expected a miracle or some supernatural manifestation; others wanted to see a complete denial of the hearsay that the Virgin had been appearing, "Don't tell me that in these times of progress and science such medieval antics would take place!"

The mothers of the three little shepherds, fearful that something might happen to their children, went to Cova da Iria but looked on from afar, hiding their faces in their aprons so they would not be recognized.

Mr. Marto, on the contrary, made himself very visible next to Jacinta. He was there to protect her but also to clear up his own doubts.

Lucia describes what happened,

> July 13, 1917—Moments after we arrived at Cova da Iria, next to the holm oak, amidst a great crowd of people, while praying the Rosary, we saw a reflection of the usual light and then Our Lady upon the tree.
>
> "What does Your Grace want of me?" I asked.
>
> "I want you to come here on the thirteenth of the next month, to continue saying the Rosary every day in honor of Our Lady of the Rosary to obtain peace in the world and the end of the war [World War I], because only she can avail you."
>
> "I wanted to ask you to tell us who you are, to work a miracle so that everyone will believe that you appear to us," I said.
>
> "Continue to come here every month. In October I will say who I am, what I want and I will perform a miracle that everybody will see so they will believe."
>
> Here I made some requests I no longer remember what they were. What I do remember is that Our Lady said that it was necessary to continue saying the Rosary to obtain graces during the year. And she continued:
>
> "Sacrifice yourselves for sinners and say very often, especially whenever you make some sacrifice:

Lucia, Francisco and Jacinta

'O Jesus, it is for Thy love, for the conversion of sinners and in reparation for the sins committed against the Immaculate Heart of Mary.'"

Upon saying these last words, she again opened her hands as in the preceding two months. The reflection appeared to penetrate into the earth and we saw, as it were, a sea of fire. Submerged in that fire were demons and souls in human shapes who resembled red-hot, black and bronze-colored embers that floated about in the blaze borne by the flames that issued from them with clouds of smoke, falling everywhere like sparks in great fires, without weight or equilibrium, amidst moans of pain and despair that horrified us and made us shake with terror (that must be when I shouted "aahhi" people said they heard). The devils had horrible and disgusting shapes of scary and unknown animals but were transparent like black burning coals. Scared and as if asking for help, we raised our eyes to Our Lady, who

Jacinta, Lucia and Francisco after the vision of hell.

said with goodness and sadness:

"You have seen hell, where the souls of poor sinners go; in order to save them, God wants to establish devotion to my Immaculate Heart in the world. If they do what I tell you, many souls will be saved and there will be peace. The war will come to an end. But if they do not stop offending God, in the reign of Pius XI a worse war will begin. When you see a night illuminated by an unknown light, know that it is the great sign that God gives you that He will punish the world for its crimes by means of war, hunger and persecutions against the Church and the Holy Father.

"To prevent it I will come to ask the consecration of Russia to my Immaculate Heart and the Communion of Reparation on the First Saturdays. If my requests are fulfilled, Russia will convert and there will be peace; if not, she will spread her errors throughout the world, promoting wars and persecutions of the Church. The good will be martyred, the

Holy Father will have much to suffer and many
nations will be annihilated. Finally, my Immaculate
Heart will triumph. The Holy Father will consecrate
Russia to me and she will be converted and the world
will be given a certain period of peace. In Portugal the
dogma of the Faith will be always preserved, etc.

"Do not tell this to anyone. But you may tell
Francisco about it.

"When you say the Rosary, after each mystery,
pray: 'O my Jesus, forgive us our sins, save us from
the fires of hell, lead all souls to heaven, especially
those in most need of thy mercy.'"[1]

An instant of silence followed, and I asked, "Is
there nothing else you wish of me?"

"No. Today I want nothing else of you."

And, as usual, she began to rise toward the east
until she disappeared in the vast distance of the firmament.

Mr. Marto recounts that when Lucia announced that Our
Lady was coming,

I could not see anything at first. But then I saw
what looked like a little grayish cloud resting on the
oak tree. The heat of the sun was suddenly less
severe. A fine fresh breeze was blowing, and it did not
seem like the height of summer. The people were
silent, terribly silent, and then I began to hear a sound,
a little buzzing sound it was, like a fly in a bottle. I
could not hear any words, but just that buzzing.

Many testimonies by people present at the apparitions tell
about the buzzing and the little cloud or the presence of gray-

---

1. "Especially those in most need of thy mercy." As Sister Lucia, understood, this
   refers to souls in greater danger of perdition.

The Third Secret

The *first part* of the secret of Fatima is the vision of Hell shown by Our Lady to the three children in the July apparition. The *second part* is Our Lady's warning of a chastisement to come if her requests are not fulfilled. However, over the decades popular usage has been to refer to the first *part* (the vision of Hell) as the *First secret,* and Our Lady's admonishing as the *Second secret.* Both *parts* or *secrets* were revealed by Sister Lucia in 1941. In addition to the first and second parts of the secret of Fatima, there is a third one, commonly called the *Third secret,* which the seer omitted in her Memoirs.

She only wrote *this third* part or *Third secret,* in January 1944, at request of the Bishop of Leiria, Dom José Alves Correia da Silva. On June 26, 2000, in accordance with specific instructions from His Holiness, Pope John Paul II, the Congregation for the Doctrine of the Faith released the text of the *Third Secret.*

This is the Vatican's official English translation of the text of the *Third Secret* as published on the Vatican Website:

J.M.J.
The third part of the secret revealed at the Cova da Iria—Fatima, on 13 July 1, 1917.

I write in obedience to you, my God, who command me to do so through his Excellency the Bishop of Leiria and through your Most Holy Mother and mine.

After the two parts which I have already explained, at the left of Our Lady and a little above, we saw an Angel with a flaming sword in his left hand; flashing, it gave out flames that looked as though they would set the world on fire; but they died out in contact with the splendor that Our Lady radiated towards him from her right hand: pointing to the earth with his right hand, the Angel cried out in a loud voice: 'Penance, Penance, Penance!'. And we saw in an immense light that is God: 'something similar to how people appear in a mirror when they pass in front of it' a Bishop dressed in White 'we had the impression that it was the Holy Father'. Other Bishops, Priests, men and women Religious going up a steep mountain, at the top of which there was a big Cross of rough-hewn trunks as of a cork-tree with the bark; before reaching there the Holy Father passed through a big city half in ruins and half trembling with halting step, afflicted with pain and sorrow, he prayed for the souls of the corpses he met on his way; having reached the top of the mountain, on his knees at the foot of the big Cross he was killed by a group of soldiers who fired bullets and arrows at him, and in the same way there died one after another the other Bishops, Priests, men and women Religious, and various lay people of different ranks and positions. Beneath the two arms of the Cross there were two Angels each with a crystal aspersorium in his hand, in which they gathered up the blood of the Martyrs and with it sprinkled the souls that were making their way to God.

Tuy-3-1-1944".

(http://www.vatican.va/roman_curia/congregations/cfaith/documents/rc_con_cfaith_doc_20000626_message-fatima_en.html)

ish or undefined white forms at times resembling doves.

What is certain is that an ambience of piety and recollection was created and that many people, even more than seeing something, somehow felt a supernatural presence. For example, in the testimony published by the Critical Documentation of Fatima (see Bibliography), Mr. Inácio Antonio Marques, speaking about the July apparition, says:

> As an unbeliever I even want to deny everything that I see, but looking on the atmosphere, I see everything is dark. It seems as if two opposing currents of air are meeting at the place, raising a cloud of dust. The weather becomes dark and I seem to hear an underground thunder. I feel that the ambience is almost supernatural, and I am afraid of being there.

CHAPTER 6
Sin and Punishment

In order to show the gravity of sin, Mary Most Holy presents its consequences: in the afterlife, eternal punishment, hell, and in this life, wars and persecutions of the Church and of the good.

At the root of sin is a form of "practical atheism." Even if he does not deny God's existence, in practice the sinner acts as if He did not exist. As he sins, man convinces himself that God will not punish him for disobeying His Law. Now then, God would not be perfect if He were not just, and He would not be just if He dispensed the same treatment to both good and bad; giving the reward of eternal happiness to those who obey His Law and to those who disobey it. That would violate the fundamental principle of justice that each person must be treated according to his deeds. Therefore, God would not be perfect. Since the notion of an imperfect God is absurd, it implies a certain doubt regarding His very existence.

In order for those innocent children to understand the extreme gravity of sin, Our Lady did not hesitate to show them its terrific final consequence: hell. Were it not for His boundless mercy—God gives special graces in special trials—one would say that gesture was an act of unspeakable cruelty. And

Shock and horror are all too evident on the faces of the three children after the vision of hell.

Sister Lucia recognizes that, were it not for those special graces and the promise they would be taken to heaven, the three would have died of fear.

When one looks at the picture of the little shepherds taken right after their vision of hell, the expression of terror and suffering on their faces is such that it gives us an idea of the terrible reality of hell.

The Mother follows the pedagogy of her Son. In His preaching on earth, Our Lord continually referred to hell and to the fact that it is eternal. Indeed, he who does not fear hell ends up not really desiring to go to heaven either. Saint Gregory the Great observes that sinners would like to live eternally in order to remain eternally in their sin.

Hell must be seen within the overall context of Catholic doctrine, which is supremely balanced, showing at the same time God's justice and mercy and the most abundant means He places at our disposal to save us. There is nothing nervous or pathological about fear of hell; instead, it gives us a wholesome and balanced fear of offending God, which affords us, still on this earth, the happiness that derives from practicing virtue. Unfortunately, today even more than at that time, hell is the great forgotten dogma.

In 1917, the First World War, which destroyed the fine flower of European youth, was raging in earnest. That year the United States sent troops to combat on the Old Continent and the rumors of war were heard in that peaceful region of Fatima, as Portugal also had troops involved in the conflict and an older half-brother of Jacinta and Francisco had been drafted.

Our Lady presented that war as a chastisement for the sins of mankind, which had fallen away from God, and she warned that if people did not amend and heed her requests, a worse war would come in the reign of Pope Pius XI and Communism, the "errors of Russia," would spread everywhere.

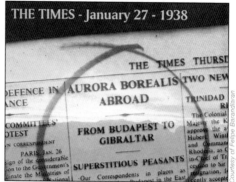

THE TIMES - January 27 - 1938

As Our Lady predicted to Lucia during the July 13th apparition, a light was seen across Europe in January of 1938. The phenomenon was reported as an Aurora Borealis. The Second World War broke out the following year.

Courtesy of Felipe Barandiaran

A few doubts arose about this prophecy, since World War II is generally considered to have started with the German invasion of Poland in 1939, already within the reign of Pius XII. In fact, when Pius XI died, in February 1939, a virtual state of war already existed, with Hitler making ever greater demands for territory and threatening the use of force. Germany had already annexed Austria on March 12, 1938, and was about to occupy Bohemia and Moravia, which were parts of Czechoslovakia, on March 15, 1939.

That is why Sister Lucia deemed the extraordinary light that illuminated the skies of Europe the night of January 25–26, 1938, during the hours of 8:45 p.m. to 1:15 a.m., a sign that the war was near.

And though Communism as a political movement is going through one of its chameleonic metamorphoses, the essence of its spirit, which is the complete abandonment of the Law of God and the rejection of a society molded according to the spirit of the Gospel, is more alive than ever. Just think of the frightful victories of the homosexual movement and the growing disintegration of the family, attacked from all quarters, including by legislation that increasingly restricts parental authority.

Hell: A Forgotten Dogma

The existence of an eternal hell is a truth of the Faith, defined by the Church in councils, symbols of Faith and documents of the Magisterium. In addition, scriptural references to it are countless, including this impressive sentence of the Divine Savior, "Depart from me, you cursed, into everlasting fire which was prepared for the devil and his angels" (Matt. 25:41).

In this affirmation, the existence of hell is unquestionable ("fire which was prepared for the devil and his angels") as well as the interminability of the fire and the separation from God ("[d]epart from Me, you cursed, into everlasting fire").

The same Evangelist recounts other statements of the Savior in which the sensible torment in hell is illustrated with the loss of the Divine Presence, exterior darkness and the weeping and gnashing of teeth. For example Jesus describes in this way the fate awaiting those who refuse him, "they will be cast out into the exterior darkness: there will be weeping and gnashing of teeth" (Matt. 8:12).

Likewise, in the parable of the wedding feast of the king's son, referring to the man without a wedding garment (that is, without innocence), Jesus says, "Bind his hands and feet, and cast him into the exterior darkness: there will be weeping and gnashing of teeth" (Matt. 22:12–13) and again concerning the unfaithful servant of the parable of the talents Jesus says, "cast him into the exterior darkness. There shall be weeping and gnashing of teeth" (Matt. 25:30).

In the parable of the wheat and the tares, Our Lord explains, "The Son of man shall send his angels, and they shall gather out of his kingdom all scandals, and them that work iniquity. And shall cast them into the furnace of fire: there shall be weeping and gnashing of teeth" (Matt. 13:41–42).

In the Gospel of Saint Mark we find another severe warning about hell. There, Our Lord insists on the fire that never goes out and the worm that does not die. These symbolize the eternity of the two main torments of Hell: one of the senses (fire) and one of loss (the worm, which represents continuous remorse and the privation of the presence of and hope in God):

"And if thy hand scandalize thee, cut it off: it is better for thee to enter into life, maimed, than having two hands to go into hell, into unquenchable fire: Where their worm dieth not, and the fire is not extinguished. And if thy foot scandalize thee, cut it off. It is better for thee to enter lame into life everlasting, than having two feet, to be cast into the hell of unquenchable fire: Where their worm dieth not, and the fire is not extinguished. And if thy eye scandalize thee, pluck it out. It is better for thee with one eye to enter into the kingdom of God, than having two eyes to be cast into the hell of fire: Where their worm dieth not, and the fire is not extinguished. For every one shall be salted with fire: and every victim shall be salted with salt." (Mark 9:42–48)

These terrible examples sufficiently demonstrate how the Divine Savior insisted on eternal punishment to prepare his listeners for conversion, and ultimately eternal salvation.

(Luiz Sérgio Solimeo, "Hell," Chap. 3 in *Life After Death According to Catholic Teaching* http://www.tfp.org/TFPForum/online_library/life_after_death/chapter_3.htm)

CHAPTER 7

A Secret and a Miracle!

If the two preceding apparitions had drawn the mockery of some, the curiosity of many and elicited movements of faith and piety in others, the announcement the seers made after the third apparition had the effect of a bombshell. Our Lady, the children said, had confided to them a secret and promised to work a miracle in October that would be seen by everyone.

A secret? What could be more appropriate to arouse human curiosity than a secret? All the more so a secret given by someone from heaven!

For superficial minds, the excitement about learning a secret and the expectation of a spectacular event are more important than their meaning or significance. But the reaction of serious and supernatural people is altogether different: A secret coming from heaven inspires respect and even wholesome fear. What message does God have in store for men?

In the Old Testament, the prophets warned the people of divine punishments because of their sins. And when the prophets were heeded by the crowds, as the Prophet Jonas was heeded by the inhabitants of Nineveh, punishment was suspended. Could it be that the secret that the Blessed Mother communicated to the little shepherds spoke of a chastisement?

In most people, however, curiosity supersedes fear and passion supersedes reflection. So, if the poor children had already suffered greatly with the previous apparitions, they were now entering a real martyrdom. They were subjected to all kinds of harassment, cajoling and threats to pry the secret out of them.

Lucia's family, who did not believe, did not bother her about it. Jacinta's and Francisco's families were dominated by the upright and balanced personality of Mr. Marto. "A secret is a secret," he would later say. If the children received a secret, they must keep it.

Right on the day following the apparition however, during the interrogation that Fatima's pastor would make after each apparition, Father Marques tried to learn the secret. But, understanding he could not force the children's consciences and seeing that his tricks did not work, he gave up.

To try and pry the secret from the children, some people would use threats, others persuasion, like some rich ladies who went to the Martos looking for the secret. One of the ladies, noticing that Jacinta was gazing with childish admiration at the beautiful bracelets she wore, offered them to her in exchange for the secret. The girl, filled with horror, said for nothing in this world would she ever part with a secret the Blessed Mother had confided to her, and that was the end of that.

To try and learn the secret, civil authorities employed threats and then force. But to delve into this we need to explain a little bit the political situation of Portugal at that time.

In the Name of Progress, a Dictatorship of Irreligion

In the name of science and progress, a wave of anticlericalism was sweeping Europe; a science and a progress whose immediate fruits had been the formidable cannons that were slaughtering the youth and destroying the beautiful cities of the Old Continent.

On February 1, 1908, the King of Portugal, Dom Carlos, and the heir prince, Dom Luis Felipe, were assassinated. The king's second son ascended to the throne with the title Dom Manuel II but was overthrown in 1910 by a revolution that established a French-style, atheist, anticlerical and socialist republic.

Religious orders were expelled, the clergy was persecuted, and wearing religious garb or ringing church bells was forbidden. The Cardinal Patriarch of Lisbon was exiled. All over the country, but particularly in smaller cities, all one had to do to land a public job was to declare oneself anti-Catholic.

A "Tinsmith" Against Fatima

Aljustrel, like its surrounding villages, was part of the Administrative Council of Vila Nova de Ourém. The Council was presided over by a virulent anticlerical, Arthur Oliveira Santos, a tinker by profession, and known for that reason by the sobriquet "The Tinsmith."

On August 10, Santos sent an official message to the parents of Lucia and Francisco and Jacinta, summoning them to appear at the Council's headquarters with the children. Mr. Marto refused to oblige his small children to go on such a tiring walk and decided to go alone, but Antonio, Lucia's father, took her along.

Santos pressured the seer to tell the secret and promise not to return to Cova da Iria. Seeing the girl would not oblige, he strongly criticized her parents and threatened future measures.

The Seers' Imprisonment

On August 13, an imposing crowd had gathered at the place

The fourth apparition of Our Lady of Fatima took place at *Valinhos*, a property belonging to one of Lucia's uncles, on August 19th.

of the apparitions. But the time was going by and the little shepherds had not shown up. People became nervous.

All of a sudden, a rumor spread, "The seers are not coming!" and "The seers have been arrested by the Administrator!"

Even so, at the time set for the apparition, many believed they had seen a small cloud approaching the holm oak and then moving away. Later, everyone heard a strong blast that caused a stampede, soon interrupted by shouts of "Miracle!" Everyone understood that the Virgin had manifested her displeasure for the absence of the seers.

What had happened?

Early in the morning, Santos, accompanied by the parish priest of Porto de Mós village, had gone to Aljustrel to the seers' house looking for them. He said he wanted to witness the apparition "like Saint Thomas, seeing to believe."

He then proposed that everyone go to the rectory for Father Marques to interrogate the children once again, which was done. As the interrogation ended, Santos told the children he would take them to Cova da Iria in his horse-drawn carriage. Unsuspectingly, they climbed up into the wagon and Mr. Marto saw it move in the right direction, but when they reached the crossroads with the main road, Santos changed course and galloped away toward Vila Nova de Ourém.

Once at the town, the seers were first taken to Santos' home, whose spouse, who practiced religion unbeknownst to her husband, treated them as well as she could and served them lunch. Then the children were taken to city hall, where they were questioned about the secret. They then returned to the Administrator's home, where they slept.

The next day, Santos decided to really terrorize them out of their wits and locked them in jail with thieves. They were not as evil as that "apostle of progress" and tried to encourage the children, to the point of saying a Rosary with them.

Finally, the iniquitous town despot took his threats to an unspeakable degree of cruelty. Deceiving those innocent children ready to believe the intimidations of adults, he demanded they tell him the secret or he would have them boiled in a cauldron of oil.

Some time having elapsed, one of the guards came calling for Jacinta first and saying the oil was already boiling, so she must tell the secret. Choosing martyrdom instead, the heroic child refused to speak and was taken away. Francisco and Lucia already imagined their little friend dead, when they came for her brother and finally for Lucia. To their great surprise and disappointment, as they wanted ardently to suffer martyrdom and go to heaven, they found themselves alive together in the same room!

The seer's abduction caused enormous popular indignation. Since they had first been taken to the rectory, the people thought the pastor had been Santos' accomplice. Tempers flared and perhaps the poor parish priest would have been killed by the furious crowd were it not for Mr. Marto's intervention, whose authority people always respected, who asked the crowd to calm down because God had allowed that event to happen.

To defend his honor, Father Marques wrote an open letter published by several Catholic publications. That was providential, as in order to justify himself he ended by narrating the whole story and thus making the Fatima events known all over the country.

On August 15, unable to hold the children any longer, Santos freed them.

Our Lady waited . . . .

Sister Lucia writes:

> [Sunday, August 19]. Walking with the sheep in the

company of Francisco and his brother João in a place called Valinhos, and feeling that something supernatural was approaching and enveloping us, we suspected that Our Lady was going to appear and were sorry that Jacinta would miss her, so we asked her brother João to go call her. Since he did not want to go, I offered him two cents, and then he ran over there.

However, with Francisco, I saw the reflection of the light that we used to call lightning; and seconds after Jacinta arrived, we saw Our Lady upon a holm oak.

"What do you want from me?"

"I want you to continue going to Cova da Iria on the thirteenth and that you continue to say the Rosary every day. In the last month I will work the miracle so that all may believe."

"What do you want to be done with the money that people leave at Cova da Iria?"

"Make two litters: one to be carried by you with Jacinta and two other girls dressed in white; and the other, by Francisco with another three boys. The money left over from making the litters is for the feast of Our Lady of the Rosary, and whatever is left from that is to help build a chapel that you will have erected."

"I want to ask you for the cure of some sick people."

"Yes; I will cure a few during the year."

And taking on a more sad appearance:

"Pray, pray a lot and do sacrifices for sinners, for many souls go to hell because there is no one to make sacrifice and pray for them."

And, as usual, she began to rise toward the east.

This was the only apparition of the Fatima series that took place outside Cova da Iria.

In the interrogation done by Father Marques on August 21,

two days after the apparition, Lucia gave the following detail, which she left out of her 1941 report, in relation to the miracle that would take place at the last apparition, "Had they not taken you to [Vila Nova de Ourém], the miracle would have been greater."

An Unknown Perfume

Jacinta took a branch of the small tree on which Our Lady had rested, in Valinhos, and showed it to her aunt, Maria Rosa, Lucia's mother. Although manifesting her usual disbelief regarding the apparitions, she smelled an unknown perfume as she took the branch to her nose.

"What perfume is this? It is not from roses, but it is pleasant."

Jacinta took the same branch to her father, who had the

In the Ourém Jail

Sister Lucia writes:

When we had been in jail for a while, the hardest thing for Jacinta was to feel abandoned by her parents; and she would say, with tears running down her cheeks, "Neither your parents nor mine ever came to see us. They no longer care about us!"

[In fact, Mr. Marto had sent two sons to find out about them.]

"Do not cry," said Francisco. "Let us offer it up to Jesus, for sinners."

And raising his little hands to heaven, he made this offer, "O my Jesus, it is for Thy love and for the conversion of sinners."

Jacinta added, "And also for the Holy Father and in reparation for the sins committed against the Immaculate Heart of Mary."

same reaction: He smelled a perfume he could not define.

"Where is this from?" he asked.

"It is a branch upon which Our Lady rested," replied Jacinta

Lucia's older sister, Maria dos Anjos, commented that from that moment on her mother's total certainty of the falseness of the apparitions was shaken.

CHAPTER 8
Like in Palestine, 2,000 Years Ago . . .

The Fatima apparitions had ceased being a local event, a strange case involving three uncultured children from the highlands, to become a national event with repercussions beyond the country's borders, among Portuguese soldiers stationed in France.

Pray to Our Lady for me

Just as people in times of old would crowd near the roads of Palestine waiting for the Divine Master to implore a cure, a consolation, a saving word, people now began to throng around the humble little shepherds as they passed by, and to kneel at their feet. In her memoirs, Sister Lucia recounts:

September 13, 1917—As the time drew near, I went there with Jacinta and Francisco passing only with difficulty through a large crowd. The roads were teeming with people, everyone wanted to see us and talk to us. No one had human respect. Many people, even ladies and gentlemen, managed to break through the crowd around us and would kneel before us asking us to present their needs to Our Lady. Others, unable to reach us, cried out from a distance, "For God's sake! Ask Our Lady to cure my invalid son!"

Another, "That She may cure mine, who's blind!"

Another, "Mine, who's deaf!"

"Let Her bring back my husband . . . "

" . . . my son, who's gone to war!"

"May She convert a sinner on my behalf!"

"That She give me health, as I have tuberculosis!"

Etc. etc.

All the miseries of mankind appeared there. Some

The three children at the foot of a cross near their parish church.

shouted from the tops of the trees they had climbed to
see us pass. We would say yes to some, stretch out our
hands to others to help raise them from the ground, as
we moved onward thanks to a few gentlemen who
opened up the way for us amidst the multitude.

Now when I read the New Testament about those
enchanting scenes of the passage of Our Lord through
Palestine, I recall the scenes that Our Lord made me
witness, still as a child, on these poor roads and paths
from Aljustrel to Fatima and Cova da Iria, and I thank
God, offering Him the faith of our good Portuguese
people. . . .

A New Apparition of the Virgin

We finally arrived at Cova da Iria, next to the holm
oak, and began to say the Rosary with the people. A
little later, we saw the reflection of light and then Our
Lady upon the tree.

"Continue to say the Rosary to obtain the end of
the war. In October Our Lord will also come, as well
as Our Lady of Sorrows and of Mount Carmel, and
Saint Joseph with the Child Jesus to bless the world.
God is happy with your sacrifices but He does not
want you to sleep with the rope [tied around the
waist]; wear it during the day.

"People have asked me to ask You for many
things: the cure of some sick persons, a deaf-mute."

"Yes, I will cure some, but not others. In October I
will work the miracle for all to believe." And beginning to rise, she disappeared as usual.

When the apparition ended, Lucia naively exclaimed, "If
you want to see Our Lady, look there," and pointed toward
the East.

In fact, many saw not the Blessed Mother but—to speak in allegorical terms—the "vehicle" that took her to heaven. . . .

"I Saw, Clearly and Distinctly, a Luminous Globe . . . "

In a letter of 1932, when he was already Vicar General of the Diocese of Leiria, Monsignor João Quaresma tells what he witnessed in September 1917 at Cova da Iria:

> On a beautiful September morning we [Father Manuel do Carmo Góis, Father Manuel Pereira da Silva and Monsignor João Quaresma] left Leiria in a rickety carriage drawn by an old horse for the spot where the much-discussed apparitions were said to take place. Father Góis found a vantage point from which we could observe events without getting too close to the place where the children were awaiting the apparition.
>
> At midday there was complete silence. One heard only the murmur of prayers. Suddenly there were sounds of jubilation and voices praising the Blessed Virgin. Arms were raised pointing to something in the sky. "Look, don't you see?"
>
> "Yes, yes I do...! " Much satisfaction on the part of those who do. There had not been a cloud in the deep blue sky and I too raised my eyes and scrutinized it in case I should be able to distinguish what others, more fortunate than I, had already claimed to have seen.
>
> With great astonishment I saw, clearly and distinctly, a luminous globe, which moved from the east to the west, gliding slowly and majestically through space. My friends also looked, and had the good fortune to enjoy the same unexpected and delightful vision. Suddenly the globe, with its extraordinary light, disappeared.

Near us was a little girl dressed like Lucia, and more or less the same age. She continued to cry out happily: "I still see it! I still see it! Now it's coming down!"

After a few minutes, about the duration of the apparitions, the child began to exclaim again, pointing to the sky, "Now it's going up again!" and she followed the globe with her eyes until it disappeared in the direction of the sun. "What do you think of the globe?" I asked my companion, who seemed enthusiastic at what he had seen. "That it was Our Lady,' he replied without hesitation.

It was my undoubted conviction also. The children had contemplated the very Mother of God, whereas we were allowed to see the means of transportation that brought her from heaven to the inhospitable waste of the Serra do Aire.

Interrogations by Canon Formigão

Also very important is the fact that, for the first time, many priests were present at that apparition, including Canon Dr. Manuel Nunes Formigão (1883–1958). That pious and cultured priest had studied in Rome at the time of Saint Pius X and received a degree in theology and canon law. On his way back to Portugal, he went by Lourdes, where he promised Our Lady to do all he could to increase devotion to her in his country.

Dr. Formigão interrogated the little shepherds and, both by their answers and, above all, their unpretentiousness and piety, was convinced they spoke the truth. He became a great apostle of Fatima, writing numerous articles and books to make the apparitions known. He was also part of the Canonical Commission appointed by the Bishop of Leiria to study the events. The Commission concluded they were authentic, thus paving the way for that prelate's official approval of the Fatima apparitions.

CHAPTER 9
The Great Miracle

The miracle that happened at Cova da Iria on October 13, 1917, when the sun "danced" in the sky, to use the expression of a newspaper at the time, was an extraordinary event of biblical dimensions comparable to Joshua's making the sun stop or to Moses dividing the waters of the Red Sea so the Jews could cross with dry feet.

A Miracle Promised in Advance

If the event itself is stupendous, perhaps no less extraordinary is the fact that it was promised three months in advance to prove that the children were telling the truth: That they really had seen Our Lady and received a message from her.

After the apparitions of August and September, the seers confirmed that in October Our Lady would work a miracle that would be seen by everyone. That announcement of a spectacular supernatural event at a time when the world had suppos-

According to renowned Fatima author William T. Walsh, the miracle of the sun was witnessed by 70,000 people and observed from several miles away.

At the Cova da Iria on October 17, 1917.

Fatima Sanctuary archive

Jacinta is carried away from the apparition site by a police officer.

edly "freed" itself from the supernatural thanks to "science" sounded like a far-fetched challenge. It simply could not happen because it would negate all the official ideology of the time—pretentious scientism, high-sounding but empty liberalism, and gross materialism.

Campaigns of Hatred

All over the country, newspapers began a bitter campaign of mockery to discredit the apparitions. Lisbon's leading daily, *O Século*, published a cartoon showing a peasant in state of revolt facing a skeleton half enveloped in a death shroud with "Hunger" written on it and the phrase, "Hunger is the one true, palpable, real apparition."

Although the multitudes of believers increased by the day, real but unspoken threats could be heard, "If the children have lied and nothing happens . . . ."

Our Lady Has Promised, She Will Fulfill

Lucia's family was very concerned about the disgrace they would be cast in if everyone's expectations were frustrated. But Mr. Marto remained calm, "Our Lady promised the miracle, she will do it."

A pious lady from a neighboring village, Dona Maria do Carmo Menezes, seeing the state of exhaustion in which the children found themselves because of the continuing interrogations, which is something Dr. Formigão had also noticed, obtained authorization from the seers' families to take them to her home so they could rest. But when people noticed the children were there, inopportune visits resumed.

The good lady, seeing many people so excited about the promise of the miracle, said to the children, "My children, if the miracle that you predict does not take place, these people are capable of burning you alive."

With a certainty given only by the

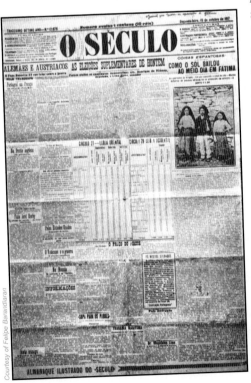

Journalist Avelino de Almeida published his first report on the apparitions on October 15th in the daily *O Século*.

Faith, they answered, "We are not afraid, because Our Lady does not deceive us. She told us that there would be a great miracle so that everyone would have to believe."

A Peaceful and Orderly Multitude

Journalist Avelino de Almeida, of the above-mentioned anti-clerical newspaper *O Século*, went to cover the event accompanied by photographer Judah Ruah. On October 15 he published in that newspaper a report with pictures that became famous. Its headline says it all, *"FRIGHTENING EVENTS! HOW THE SUN DANCED IN FATIMA AT NOON."*

Except for a few ironies and innuendos his general description of the events is very well done and objective. Avelino de Almeida simply describes what he saw. Because he is a witness against his will, we will draw from his report the general description of what happened; then we will transcribe, as in the previous apparitions, Sister Lucia's own description.

From dawn, all roads leading to Cova da Iria and adjacent fields were taken over by a huge multitude. After consulting with many other persons, the journalist calculated thirty to forty thousand people were present, while other sources spoke of seventy to eighty thousand.

It was an orderly, peaceful and pious crowd. There were neither tumults nor lamentations, but hope. They would go in groups, some singing religious hymns, others praying the Rosary. And the strong rain that started to fall did not cool off their enthusiasm or slow them down.

The journalist says there was a kind of mystical, supernatural atmosphere.

"I Am the Lady of the Rosary"

Before narrating the miracle of the sun, let us see how Sister

Lucia recounts the last apparition of the Fatima cycle.[1]

On October 13, 1917, we left home quite early to make up for possible delays along the way. The people were there en masse; the rain, torrential. My mother, fearing that would be the last day of my life, with her heart dilacerated by the uncertainty of what was going to happen wanted to accompany me. Along the way were repeated scenes of the past, more numerous and touching. Not even the very muddy roads prevented those people from kneeling down in a very humble and supplicating attitude. Having arrived at Cova da Iria, next to the holm oak, led by an interior movement I asked the people to close their umbrellas for us to say the Rosary. A little later we saw the reflection of the light and then, Our Lady upon the holm oak.

"What do you want from me?"

"I want to tell you to have a little chapel built here in my honor, as I am the Lady of the Rosary, and to continue saying the Rosary every day. The war will come to an end and the military will soon return home."

"I had many things to ask you: if you could cure some sick people, convert some sinners etc."

"Some, yes; others, no. They need to make

---

1. Fatima specialists are not in agreement about the meaning of the promise Our Lady made in the first apparition of May 13, that she would return to the Cova da Iria a seventh time. Would it have been the private apparition to Sister Lucia on June 16, 1921 when she was about to leave for the city of Porto to study with the Dorothean sisters? Or should this one also have been public since, as others consider, the six previous apparitions were public? The fact that the seers have died does not alter the question since Our Lady did not say explicitly that She would appear to them, but only that She would return: "I will return here a seventh time." Since we are lacking decisive elements to clear up the matter we consider it an open question.

amends, to ask forgiveness for their sins."

And taking on a sad aspect, "Do not offend Our Lord anymore, Who is already much offended."

And opening her hands, she made them reflect upon the sun. And while she was rising, the reflection of her own light continued to be projected on the sun.

This is the reason why I called out for the people to look at the sun. My goal was not to call their attention to it, as I didn't even notice their presence. I only did it led by an interior movement that impelled me to do it.

Multiple Apparitions

As Our Lady disappeared in the vast distance of the firmament, we saw next to the sun, Saint Joseph with the Child and Our Lady dressed in white with a blue mantle. Saint Joseph and the Child appeared to bless the world with gestures of their hands in the shape of a cross. A while later, this apparition having vanished, I saw Our Lord and Our Lady, who

Thousands of pilgrims came from all over to witness the miracle promised by Our Lady.

appeared to be Our Lady of Sorrows. Our Lord appeared to bless the world in the same way as Saint Joseph. This apparition also vanished and it seemed to me I saw Our Lady in a form similar to Our Lady of Mount Carmel.

The Miracle of the Sun

Let us now take up the description of Avelino de Almeida, who saw everything with skeptical but keenly observant eyes. This is the description of the miracle of the sun published by the Lisbon newspaper *O Século* two days after the event.

The point of the low land of Fatima where the Virgin is said to have appeared to the little shepherds of the village of Aljustrel can be seen from a long stretch of the road to Leiria, where the vehicles that brought the pilgrims and curiosity seekers were parked. Someone counted more than one hundred automobiles and more than one hundred bicycles, and it would be impossible to count the innumerable vehicles cluttering the road, one of them a bus from Torres Novas with people from all layers of society.

But the bulk of the pilgrims, thousands of creatures who had come from many miles away to join the faithful of various provinces such as Alentejo, Algarve, Minho and Beira, congregated around the small holm oak which, as the little shepherds put it, the vision had chosen as its pedestal; it could be considered the center of an ample circle around whose borders other spectators and devotees assembled. Seen from the road, the ensemble is simply fantastic. Many of the prudent peasants, protected by enormous hats, accompany the spiritual hymns and decades of the Rosary while nibbling on their poor fare.

No one fears to walk through this mushy clay to see up close the holm oak over which was built a rude portal on which two lanterns flicker. . . . As groups singing praise of the Virgin take turns, a frightened rabbit sprinting out of the woods barely manages to get the attention of a half-dozen youngsters who catch up with it and bludgeon it unconscious. . . .

And what about the little shepherds? Lucia, 10, the seer, and her small companions Francisco, 9, and Jacinta, 7, still have not arrived. Their presence is noticed a half-hour before the time set for the apparition. The little girls, crowned with garlands of flowers, are led to the place where the portal stands. The rain falls incessantly but no one despairs. Cars with latecomers arrive on the road. Groups of faithful kneel in the mud and Lucia asks and orders them to close their umbrellas. The order is passed on and obeyed immediately without the least reluctance. Many people find themselves, as it were, in ecstasies; many are touched, prayer has paralyzed their dry lips; many seem dazed, with their hands together and eyes wide open; people seem to feel and touch the supernatural. . . .

The child says that the Lady spoke to her once again and the sky, still dark, begins to clear up on high; the rain stops and one feels the sun will flood with light that landscape which the wintry morning had made even sadder. . . .

The "old time" [official time] is the one that matters for this crowd, which impartial and cultured people completely alien to mystical influences calculate in about thirty or forty thousand creatures. . . . Many pilgrims say the miraculous manifestation, the visible sign announced, is about to happen... And then one witnesses a spectacle unique and unbelievable for someone not there to see it. From the top of the road, where cars are parked and hundreds of people gather who do not want to brave the mud, one sees the huge crowd turn toward the sun, now freed from the clouds, at its zenith. The sun resembles a plate of opaque silver and one can look at it without any strain. It does not burn or blind. One would say an eclipse is taking place. Then a huge roar comes from the crowd and those closer to the place cry out, "Miracle, miracle! Marvel, marvel!"

As the peasants typically put it, the sun "danced," shook and made abrupt movements outside all cosmic laws as those people filled with awe, with an attitude that recalls biblical times, heads uncovered, looked up into the blue with their fascinated eyes. . . . It is close to three o'clock p.m.

CHAPTER 10
A Sign of Contradiction

The prophet Simeon, holding the Child Jesus in his arms during his presentation at the Temple, prophesied that He would be a sign of contradiction—of salvation for some who would accept Him and of perdition for others who would reject Him. In relation to Him the intimate thoughts of men would be uncovered, revealing who each man really is before God. And turning to Mary Most Holy he completed his prophecy by saying, "And thy own soul a sword shall pierce, that, out of many hearts, thoughts may be revealed" (Luke 2:35).

Fatima, a Choice for Christ or Against Christ

Such has been the history of men ever since—the history of acceptance or rejection of the salvation brought by Our Lord Jesus Christ and of the merciful intercession of his Blessed Mother.

Fatima is one of those occasions in which men are called publicly to opt for or against Our Lord and his Blessed Mother; between the Faith, which demands humility, and the belief in an atheistic pseudoscience that caters to human pride.

One Cannot Deny That the Sun Danced at Fatima

The miracle of the sun was witnessed by thousands of people

in addition to the crowd gathered at the Cova da Iria. It was actually seen in an area of about six hundred square miles. It is simply impossible to deny such a spectacular phenomenon witnessed by so many people at the same time.

Furthermore, many witnesses were not illiterate peasants or priests who were presumably biased. Among the testimonies presented by Father DeMarchi and by Mr. John Haffert, who questioned hundreds of people from all social classes who saw the miracle, we find physicians such as the ophthalmologist Dr. Domingos Pinto Coelho; engineers like Dr. Mario Godinho; a professor at the famous University of Coimbra, Dr. Almeida Garret; lawyers as Dr. Carlos de Azevedo Mendes, and so forth.[1]

Journalist Avelino de Almeida himself, who had previously written satirical articles in the anticlerical newspaper *O Século*, impressed with what he witnessed at Fatima wrote a very faithful report, though without accepting the event's supernatural character.

The Hostile Campaign Continues

As usual, when liberals run out of arguments, all that's left is violence. In the name of freedom naturally. That way, they reveal the "thoughts of their hearts."

So it was that a violent campaign against Fatima was unleashed in the anticlerical press everywhere, promoted by the "partisans of progress and liberty."

On October 23, as reported by the daily *Diário de Notícias*, a band of liberals from Vila Nova de Ourém went to Cova da Iria in the still of the night and hacked down the tree of the apparitions. When Lucia heard about it she ran to the

---

1. A new edition of the admirable book by John Haffert, *Meet the Witnesses—of The Miracle of the Sun*, was published by The American Society for the Defense of Tradition, Family and Property.

place and, much to her joy, she saw they had cut down the wrong tree, one close to the holm oak on which Our Lady had landed. The latter, which had been reduced to a trunk because the faithful had taken all its branches as relics, remained standing there.

Taking to Santarém the bits and pieces of the little tree and the adornments the faithful had placed in the area, the anticlericals began to make shameful parodies of it but had to stop owing to the general indignation of the people, including non-churchgoers.

The Apparitions Cease, Pilgrimages Increase

When the apparitions ceased, pilgrimages to the place continued. That caused a great financial loss for Lucia's family, as it was no longer possible to plant anything in the whole area of Cova da Iria.

The faithful would leave offers in species and in money, collected by Maria Carreira, the zealous devotee of the apparitions, to fulfill the Blessed Mother's request to have a chapel built there in honor of Our Lady of the Rosary. For that reason, the good lady became known as "Maria da Capelinha" or "Mary of the Little Chapel."

In 1919, with the authorization of Lucia's mother and the discreet acquiescence of the parish priest of Fatima, who could not commit himself until the Religious Authority made a pronouncement on the matter, the construction of the little chapel started.

Restoration of the Diocese of Leiria

The diocese of Leiria, to which the village belonged, had been created in the 16th century and was suppressed at the end of the 19th century. That placed Fatima under the jurisdiction of the faraway Patriarchate of Lisbon. In January 1918, the

Holy See restored the diocese but the new bishop, Dom José Alves Correia da Silva, was appointed only in 1920.

As soon as he was installed, prodded by Dr. Formigão, the new bishop took an interest in Fatima and opened an ecclesiastical inquiry about the matter. Already on October 13, 1921, he authorized the celebration of a Mass at the chapel of the apparitions.

The Chapel of the Apparitions Is Blown Up

The Church's enemies again reacted violently. On March 6, 1922, the little chapel at Cova da Iria was destroyed by a powerful bomb. On May 13, as a response, a pilgrimage of reparation took place with the presence of over 60,000 people from all regions of Portugal. In December, reconstruction of the chapel started.

Thus, in spite of the violence of the adversaries, devotion to Our Lady of Fatima was victoriously gaining ground.

A very important development took place when Pope Pius XI, receiving the students of the Portuguese College in Rome on January 9, 1929, gave each one of them two holy cards of Our Lady of Fatima: one for them, the other to be sent to their families. In October 1929, at the request of that College's president, the Pope himself blessed a statue of Our Lady of Fatima sculpted by Portuguese artist José Tedim for the College's chapel.

These events are related in the Report of the Canonical Commission of the Diocese of Leiria, which concluded that the apparitions were authentic.

Finally, on October 13, 1930, Bishop José Alves Correia da Silva published a pastoral letter approving devotion to Our Lady of Fatima. Previously, in 1928, he had already approved construction of the Basilica of Fatima, for which he had purchased the plots at Cova da Iria.

In a short time the devotion spread throughout the world; and that little corner of Portugal, hidden in the Serra do Aire, became one of the world's premier centers of Catholic pilgrimage.

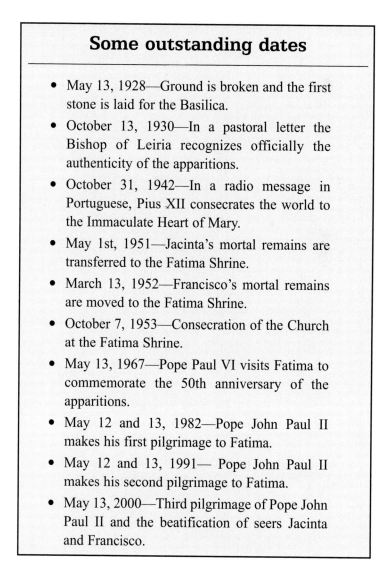

Some outstanding dates

- May 13, 1928—Ground is broken and the first stone is laid for the Basilica.
- October 13, 1930—In a pastoral letter the Bishop of Leiria recognizes officially the authenticity of the apparitions.
- October 31, 1942—In a radio message in Portuguese, Pius XII consecrates the world to the Immaculate Heart of Mary.
- May 1st, 1951—Jacinta's mortal remains are transferred to the Fatima Shrine.
- March 13, 1952—Francisco's mortal remains are moved to the Fatima Shrine.
- October 7, 1953—Consecration of the Church at the Fatima Shrine.
- May 13, 1967—Pope Paul VI visits Fatima to commemorate the 50th anniversary of the apparitions.
- May 12 and 13, 1982—Pope John Paul II makes his first pilgrimage to Fatima.
- May 12 and 13, 1991— Pope John Paul II makes his second pilgrimage to Fatima.
- May 13, 2000—Third pilgrimage of Pope John Paul II and the beatification of seers Jacinta and Francisco.

CHAPTER 11
Expiatory Victims

With the generosity typical of the innocence of their age, the three children accepted the Blessed Mother's invitation to suffer for the conversion of sinners. Furthermore, Jacinta and Francisco offered their own lives, while Lucia would have to stay on earth to fulfill a special mission.

The Supreme Wisdom of the "Folly of the Cross"

Since the Angel had begun to prepare them, but above all after the first apparition of the "beautiful Lady," the children acquired an eagerness for sacrifice and humiliations. That was not owing to a pathological condition, but on the contrary, to a superior wisdom that Saint Paul calls the "folly of the cross" (*cf.* 1 Corinthians 1:18–25). It is an ardent form of charity, fruit of an intense love of God and a vibrant Faith animated by works.

Having seen hell, where sinners go, the seers understood the supreme misfortune of eternal perdition and made themselves expiatory victims, to placate offended divine justice in order to save souls.

Love of God Generates Love for Souls

It is quite obvious that this heroic disposition is the fruit of special graces to which the children corresponded generously.

God communicates his love to the soul with such intensity that the soul becomes transformed with divine love, forgetful of self and eager to bear the redeeming suffering of Our Lord Jesus Christ and the sorrows of Mary. This is not suffering for the sake of suffering but to quench that thirst for the salvation of souls communicated by grace.

It is impossible to recount here everything that turned Francisco and Jacinta into heroes of penance for sinners, as the Church recognized at their memorable ceremony of beatification presided by Pope John Paul II at the Fatima Shrine on May 13, 2000.

Some Examples of Penance

For lack of space, we will mention only a few episodes and the words of the two little siblings, taken mostly from *The Memoirs of Sister Lucia*.

"Poor people, we will pray and make sacrifice for them!"

Despite their tender age, the three children acquired a very lively understanding of the admirable dogma of the Communion of Saints: I "rejoice in my sufferings for you," says Saint Paul to the Colossians, "and fill up those things that are wanting of the sufferings of Christ, in my flesh, for his body, which is the church" (Col. 1:24).

Jacinta thought continuously about the vision of hell, the suffering of hardened sinners there, but above all about the eternity of the punishment, and she would comment with childish candor, "Poor people! We will pray and make many sacrifices for them!"

This zeal for souls, for the conversion of sinners, led them to be inventive as to how they would sacrifice for them. One day, Lucia found a rope and proposed they cut it in three pieces so each of them could wear one around their waist to do penance.

Torment of Hunger

Francisco was the most inventive in this matter. Lucia narrates:

Francisco quickly discovered a good sacrifice.

"Let's give our lunch to the sheep and make the sacrifice of skipping it!"

In a few minutes, our lunch had all been distributed to the flock. And thus we spent the day fasting like the most austere Carthusian monk.

Later they found something better, to give their lunch to poor children they found along the way, so they started doing that daily.

But how did they feed themselves? "There were some holm oaks and some oak trees. The acorns were still pretty green, but I said we could eat them," Lucia explains. And she concludes, "That was our nourishment in those days: pine nuts, roots, berries, mushrooms and some things we harvested at the roots of the pine trees, whose name escapes me at the moment; or fruits, if there were some nearby on some property of our parents."

How not to think, as we read this, of the great penitents who inhabited the Egyptian desert during the early Church?

Torment of Thirst

Once, beside herself with thirst, Lucia asked for water at a nearby house. She brought back a jar, giving it to Francisco to drink first, but he said he wanted to offer the sacrifice of thirst for sinners. In spite of a terrible headache, Jacinta decided to do the same. In the end, not even Lucia drank, pouring the water into a hollow in a stone for the sheep to drink.

Moral Sufferings

In addition to the voluntarily chosen physical torments, they had moral torments, at times even more terrible.

When under arrest at Ourém, Lucia explains,

> They gathered us again in a room of the jail and said they would soon come for us, to have us fried; Jacinta walked up to a window from where one could see the cattle fair. At first I thought she was just entertaining herself with the view, but soon I noticed she was actually crying. I went to bring her close to me and asked why she was crying.

"Because," she answered, "we will die without
even seeing our fathers and mothers once again!"

And with tears running down her face, "I wanted at
least to see my mother!"

"Then you don't want to offer up this sacrifice for
the conversion of sinners?"

"I do, I do."

And with tears on her face and hands, and with her
eyes turned to heaven, she makes the offering, "O my
Jesus, it is for Thy love, for the conversion of sinners,
for the Holy Father and in reparation for the sins committed against the Immaculate Heart of Mary."

In October 1918, when one year had elapsed since the last
apparition, Jacinta fell ill and, a little later, so did Francisco. It
was the final preparation for Our Lady to fulfill her promise to
take them to heaven soon.

"Our Lady Came to See Us . . ."

One day, when Lucia went to visit her little cousin, she told her:

"Our Lady came to see us and said she will come
to take Francisco to heaven very soon. And She
asked me if I still wanted to convert more sinners. I
told Her yes. She said I would be going to a hospital
where I would have much to suffer; that I should suffer for the conversion of sinners, in reparation for the
sins against the Immaculate Heart of Mary, and for
the love of Jesus. I asked if you were coming with
me. She said no. This is the hardest part for me. She
said my mother would take me and then I would stay
there alone!"

On another occasion, she said to Lucia:

"[Our Lady] told me that I am going to Lisbon, to
another hospital: that I will not see you again, nor my

parents, and that after suffering a lot I will die alone, that I should not be afraid because She will go there to take me to heaven."

The Death of Francisco: "Goodbye, See You in Heaven!"

Lucia continues:

> When the moment arrived for her little brother to depart to heaven, [Jacinta] made her recommendations:
>
> "Give my best to Our Lord and Our Lady and tell them I will suffer all they want to convert sinners and make reparation to the Immaculate Heart of Mary."

Francisco's death was one of a warrior who is ready to make the supreme sacrifice of his life for the good of a cause. Having sacrificed for the conversion of sinners, he now also accepted death for the same end.

When he was about to die, he sent for Lucia and asked her tell him the sins she had seen him commit; and then he asked Lucia to also ask Jacinta, who was sick in another room, to do him the same favor, for, he said with all simplicity, "I am going to confession to receive communion and then die."

Sister Lucia's narration continues:

> As night fell, I bid farewell to him.

Francisco Marto's bedroom in his house in Aljustrel, where he died on April 4, 1919.

"Goodbye, Francisco! If you go to heaven tonight, do not forget me, you hear?"

"No, I won't forget you, you can be at ease."

And grabbing my right hand, he squeezed it strongly for a good while, looking at me with tears in his eyes.

"Do you want anything else?" I asked him, with tears running down my face as well.

"No," he answered, with a weak voice.

Since that scene was becoming far too moving, my aunt told me to leave the room.

"Goodbye, then, Francisco! See you in heaven!"

"Goodbye, see you in heaven!"

And heaven drew near. He flew there the next day, in the arms of his celestial Mother."

Francisco died on April 4, 1919 at 10:00 PM. He was almost 11 years old.

Jacinta Dies Alone at a Lisbon Hospital

Jacinta went to a hospital in Ourém, without getting any better. She returned to Aljustrel.

A renowned physician from Lisbon and a fervent Catholic, wishing to make a pilgrimage to Fatima, passed by Santarém, where he invited Dr. Formigão to go with him. That was providential to fulfill the will of Our Lady, for both, when visiting

Courtesy of Felipe Barandiaran

Jacinta Marto's bedroom in her house in Aljustrel.

Dona Estefânia Hospital where Jacinta died.

Jacinta, saw that she was in a very delicate state and had to undergo a surgery at a Lisbon hospital.

Knowing the prophecy about her daughter's death, and having seen the useless suffering she had born at the Ourém hospital, her parents did not want to allow a new attempt. The doctor and priest showed them that, even if her death was the will of the Mother of God, they needed to exhaust all human resources.

So it was because of this that the little Fatima seer, barely 10 years old, went to "die alone" in Lisbon on February 20, 1920, at 10:30 p.m. Despite her having died from purulent tuberculosis, her body, exposed at a church for a while, exuded a suave perfume.

The Baron of Alvaiázere, from Ourém, who since the October miracle

On September 12, 1935, the mortal remains of Jacinta, who died in 1920, were exhumed. Her face was found to be incorrupt.

Jacinta's Prophecies

In addition to the communications received during Our Lady's apparitions at Cova da Iria, Jacinta had many private apparitions of the Virgin and received countless revelations.

About the Pope

"One day," Lucia tells, "we went to spend our nap time next to the well of my parents. Jacinta sat on the slabs of the well; Francisco went with me to look for wild honey in the bushes of a nearby ravine. A little time having elapsed, Jacinta called out to me, "Did you not see the Holy Father?"

"No!"

"I don't know how it happened! I saw the Holy Father in a very large house, kneeling before a table, with his face in his hands, crying. Outside the house were many people, some of whom cast stones at him, others cursed him and said many ugly words. Poor Holy Father! We have to pray a lot for him."

"On another occasion," Lucia continues, "we went to [the place known as] Loca do Cabeço. Having arrived there, we prostrated ourselves on the ground, saying the prayers to the Angel. A while later, Jacinta rises and calls out to me, "Don't you see so many roads and so many ways filled with people crying with hunger and having nothing to eat? And the Holy Father in a church before the Immaculate Heart of Mary, praying? And so many people praying with him?"

Fashions

Mother Godinho, who directed the Lisbon Orphanage where Jacinta stayed before dying at the hospital, carefully wrote down the words of the holy girl.

Two of her notes are outstandingly important today. The first says, "The sins which cause most souls to go to hell are the sins of the flesh." With a directly supernatural illumination, that totally innocent, barely ten-year-old girl repeats what Saint Alphonsus Liguori says, that it is sins against chastity "that fill hell with souls."

When Mother Godinho asked Jacinta if she understood what it meant to be "pure," she answered, "I do. To be pure in body is to keep chastity. To be pure in soul is not to commit sins, not to look at what one should not see . . . ."

The other, rather prophetic statement, is, "Fashions will much offend Our Lord." It is well to recall here that modesty is the outer defense of chastity, the walls that defend the castle, as well as the gardens that adorn the palace.

The correct question, when it comes to fashion, is not what is the extreme limit at which one is allowed to arrive, but how can one's attire more clearly manifest love of modesty and of the virtue of purity.

had become not only an ardent devotee of Fatima but a friend and adviser of Mr. Marto's, offered his family's tomb, where the seer's body was buried.

Today, the remnants of both Francisco and Jacinta rest at the Basilica of Fatima.

Lucia dos Santos (standing) next to her cousin Jacinta Marto.

CHAPTER 12
"Will I Stay Here Alone?"

At the second apparition, in June, Our Lady promised to take Francisco and Jacinta to heaven soon. But in relation to Lucia, she said, "But you will remain here for some time yet. Jesus wishes to use you in order to make me known and loved. He wishes to establish devotion to my Immaculate Heart in the world."

Lucia asked this anguished question, "Will I stay here alone?"

To which the Mother of God answered maternally, "No, daughter. Does that make you suffer much? Do not be dismayed. I will never forsake you. My Immaculate Heart will be your refuge and the road that will lead you to God."

That was the vocation assigned to Sister Lucia. Whereas to her little cousins the apparitions were, so to speak, the end of their lives, to her they were merely the beginning of a long journey that ended on February 13, 2005 at the age of 97.

Multiple Sufferings

The Mother of God instructed Lucia to learn how to read. That was part of her vocation, because she would have to serve as intermediary for new communications from heaven.

Her life was not easy. For a long time, her mother, whom she admired and loved intensely, had not accepted the veracity of the apparitions. And with her resolute temperament, she had done everything to make Lucia recant, to the point of hitting Lucia's back with a broomstick.

The family's economic decline had already started before the supernatural manifestations because of her father's ineptness and drinking habits. Later, the continuous influx of curious people and pilgrims made the family's life almost impossible and destroyed the plantations at Cova da Iria. In July of 1919, Lucia's father died.

With the Dorothean Sisters

With meritorious prudence, the bishop of Leiria deemed it necessary to take the child away from the indiscreet eyes of Fatima devotees and curiosity seekers. In 1921, he obtained authorization from Lucia's mother to have Lucia moved to the city of Porto, to the Vilas Asylum directed by the Dorothean Sisters. There, while able to have peace, she would learn to read and write, and her identity would be kept secret.

Having chosen religious life, in 1925 Lucia joined that same Congregation of the Dorothean Sisters as a postulant. She then went to Tuy, a Spanish city on the border with Portugal where the postulants of the Congregation had been transferred because of the anticlerical Revolution of 1910. In 1928, she professed in that Congregation and entered it with the name Sister Maria das Dores.

In 1948, Lucia received papal license to become a Carmelite nun at the Carmel of Coimbra. She then took the name Sister Maria Lucia of the Immaculate Heart and remained at that convent until her death in 2005.

This is a short chronological sketch of the life of Sister Lucia, the privileged interlocutor of the Virgin at the Fatima apparitions.

A full-blown biography of Sister Lucia still needs to be written; and given the innumerable events to which she was linked, it would require a careful and well-documented research that still has not been done. However, the Blessed Mother, who promised to take her to heaven, certainly assisted her with special graces till the end.

Later on we will delve into the graces and revelations that Sister Lucia received, related with the Fatima promises.

CHAPTER 13
Devotion of Reparation to the Immaculate Heart

At the third apparition, on July 13, 1917, Our Lady announced that she would come to ask for the consecration of Russia to her Immaculate Heart and for the Communion of Reparation of the five First Saturdays. Since she asked first for the devotion of the First Saturdays in 1925 and then in 1929 the consecration, we will discuss these in that order as well.

The Devotion of the First Saturdays

On December 10, 1925, at the House of the Dorothean Sisters at Pontevedra, Sister Lucia had a vision. She herself narrates it, using the third person out of humility:

> On 12-10-1925, the Blessed Mother appeared to [Sister Lucia] and beside her, suspended on a luminous cloud, a Boy on whose shoulder the Blessed Mother rested her hand and at the same time, in her other hand, a heart surrounded with thorns.
>
> At the same time, the Boy said, "Have pity on the Heart of your Most Holy Mother which is covered with thorns with which ingrate men pierce it at every moment with no one to make an act of reparation to pull them out."
>
> Then, the Virgin said, "See, my daughter, My Heart surrounded with thorns with which ingrates pierce Me at every moment with blasphemies and ingratitude. You, at least, make sure to console me and say that all those who for five months, on the first Saturday, go to confession, receive Communion, say five decades of the Rosary and keep me company for 15 minutes meditating on the mysteries of the Rosary, with the purpose of making reparation to Me, I promise to assist them at the hour of death with all the

graces necessary for the salvation of their souls."

Therefore, Mary Most Holy's request is that on the First Saturday of five consecutive months, one confess and receive Communion; say five decades of the Rosary; meditate during 15 minutes on the mysteries of the Rosary; all this with the purpose of making reparation to the Immaculate Heart of Mary for the sins of men.

As Sister Lucia explained, it is not necessary to meditate on all the mysteries but to meditate each Saturday about one or more mysteries.

As a reward to those who practice this devotion, Our Lady promises to assist them at the hour of death; and grant them, at that supreme moment, all the graces necessary for salvation.

Some days later, Sister Lucia wrote a report on this vision in a letter to Monsignor Manuel Pereira Lopes, who had been her confessor while she resided at the Asylum of Vilar in the city of Porto.

In a new apparition of the Child Jesus, on February 15, 1926, Sister Lucia asked if finding it difficult to go to confession on the same Saturday one could fulfill the request by going some other day. Jesus answered, "Yes, it can be on many other [days] as long as, when they receive Me, they be in [the state of] grace and have the intention of making reparation to the Immaculate Heart of Mary."

Sister Lucia asked, "My Jesus, what about those who forget to formulate that intention?"

Jesus answered, "They can do it in the next confession, taking advantage of the first occasion to go to confession."

In a letter of June 12, 1930 to her confessor, answering his questions about the First Saturdays Devotion, in particular, "Why are they five Saturdays rather than nine or seven, in honor of the sorrows of Our Lady?" Sister Lucia explained:

> Staying in the chapel with Our Lord part of the night of the twenty-ninth to the thirtieth of the month of May 1930, and speaking to Our Lord, I suddenly felt more intimately possessed by the divine Presence; and if I am not mistaken, the following was revealed to me, "My daughter, the reason is simple. There are five kinds of offenses and blasphemies perpetrated against the Immaculate Heart of Mary: blasphemies against her Immaculate Conception; against her virginity; against her divine maternity, at the same time refusing to accept her as the Mother of men; those who publicly try to instill indifference, scorn and even hatred toward this Immaculate Mother in the hearts of children; and those who insult her directly in Her sacred images."

After much insistence by Sister Lucia through her Superior and her confessor, on September 13, 1939 the bishop of Leiria published the appeal of the Blessed Virgin Mary for the Communion of Reparation of the First Saturdays.

Devotion to the Immaculate Heart of Mary

Devotion to the Immaculate Heart of Mary is very ancient in the Church, and like the devotion to the Sacred Heart of Jesus, it exalts the whole person of the Virgin but especially that which she has of most noble, symbolically represented by her Heart.

The Heart of Mary represents her mentality as the Mother of God and her love for God and men. Saint John Eudes (1601–1680), who spread this devotion very much, along with devotion to the Sacred Heart of Jesus, finds in the Gospel of Saint Luke a reference to the Immaculate Heart.

Narrating how the shepherds were advised by the angels of the birth of the Savior and went to adore the child, and what the angels had said, Saint Luke concludes, "But Mary kept all these words, pondering them in her heart" (Luke 2:19).

The same Evangelist makes a similar comment about the episode in which the Child Jesus was lost and then found at the Temple, "And his mother kept all these words in her heart" (Luke 2:51).

Saint Pius X and the Communion of Reparation

Communion on the First Saturdays in honor of Our Lady was not a novelty. On June 13, 1912, five years before the Blessed Mother made the request at the third apparition in Fatima, Saint Pius X granted new indulgences to the First Saturdays Devotion insisting very much on the intention of making reparation:

> Pius X, pope by the grace of divine Providence, in order to promote devotion among the faithful to the glorious and immaculate Mother of God, and to favor the pious desire of the faithful to make reparation for the execrable blasphemies uttered against her august name and the heavenly prerogatives of that blessed Virgin, has deigned to grant a plenary indulgence, applicable to the souls of the deceased, on the first Saturday of the month, to all those who on that day shall confess, receive communion, and make particu-

lar exercises of devotion in honor of the blessed Virgin
Mary in a spirit of reparation as indicated above.

In Short

The Communion of Reparation on the Five First Saturdays,
as Our Lady asked Sister Lucia, is a devotion filled with the
spirit of reparation; love of the Eucharist and of the Sacrament
of Confession; love of the Immaculate Heart of Mary; and love
of the Rosary and of meditation.

It is an excellent means to maintain ourselves in the state of
grace in the neopagan world in which we live, in addition to
giving us hope for eternal salvation.

CHAPTER 14
"Russia Will Already Have Scattered her Errors Throughout the World"

The request for the consecration of Russia to the Immaculate Heart of Mary was made on June 13, 1929, the 12th anniversary of the second apparition. As Sister Lucia recounts, she was making a vigil of prayers alone in the chapel between 11 p.m. and midnight, when she had a symbolic vision about the Most Blessed Trinity and the Redemption.

The Solemnity of the Request

Suddenly, the whole chapel was illuminated with a supernatural light and on the altar appeared a cross that went all the way to the ceiling. In a brighter light one saw, on the upper part of the cross, the face of a man and his torso down to his waist, on his chest a dove and, nailed to the cross, the body of another man. A little below the waist [of the crucified], suspended in the air, one saw a Chalice and a large Host upon which were falling some drops of blood that ran down the face of the crucified and from a wound in his chest. Running down the Host, those drops fell inside the Chalice. Under the right arm of the cross was Our Lady with her Immaculate Heart in her hand (it was Our Lady of Fatima with her Immaculate Heart in her left hand, without sword or roses but with a crown of thorns and flames). Under the left arm [of the cross] large letters resembling crystalline waters running down on top of the altar, formed the words "Grace and Mercy."

The seer understood that it was an allusion to the mystery of the Most Holy Trinity, about which, she says, she received insights that she was not allowed to communicate.

In that context full of mystery and grandeur, the Mother of God addressed her, saying, "The moment has arrived when God asks the Holy Father to make, in union with all the bishops of the world, the consecration of Russia to my Immaculate Heart, promising to save [Russia] by this means."

The Advance of Socialism

The request could not have been made in a more solemn and imperative fashion. Nor could the moment be more opportune. In 1929, Communism had already consolidated its power in Russia and spread to the whole world through parties directed by Moscow. Russia (or Communism) was "spreading its errors throughout the world."

In Mexico, the Church was being persecuted by revolutionary socialist governments; in France, the radical government prepared to sign the Franco-Soviet accord of mutual assistance; in Spain, a socialist republic was about to be installed with churches being set on fire, persecutions and slaughter of Catholics and the clergy, and a bloody Civil War.

Although Nazism and the Fascist movements that appeared at that time were presented as political enemies of Communism, their ideological underpinning was also socialist—State preeminence over the individual, total control over education and the economy, the worship of force, and the amoral tenet that the end justifies the means. Above all, Nazism and Fascism shared pagan materialism and naturalism, which denies the supernatural order and transforms man into a "superman" or "demiurge."

Pope Pius XI Receives the Request
for the Consecration

Sister Lucia, as she herself confirmed, passed Our Lady's request on to her confessor, who in turn forwarded it to Pope

Pope Pius XI (1922-1939) was the pope Our Lady refered to when speaking to Lucia during the July 13th apparition.

Pius XI. Indeed, in a letter written to Pope Pius XII in 1940, she says about that communication:

> In 1929, Our Lady, in another apparition, asked for the consecration of Russia to Her Immaculate Heart, promising by that means to prevent the propagation of its errors, and its conversion.
>
> Some time later, I informed my confessor of Our Lady's request. His Reverence employed some means to have it forwarded to His Holiness Pius XI.

Likewise, on February 3, 1946, during an interview with Father Hubert Jongen, a young Dutch Montfortian priest, he asked if Pius XI had known about the request. Sister Lucia answered, "Father José Bernardo Gonçalves [my confessor] . . . informed His Grace the Bishop of Leiria about everything, and managed for the request to come to the knowledge of H.H. Pius XI."

The next year, she gave an almost identical response to Father Thomas McGlynn, O.P., an American priest. He asked, "Was this wish made known to the Holy Father at that time?" Sister Lucia replied, "I told my confessor; he informed the Bishop of Leiria. After a while my confessor said that the communication had been sent to the Holy Father."

The Consecration Was Not Made at the Proper Time

We do not have elements to know the reasons why Pope Pius XI did not make the requested consecration, all the more so since he believed in the authenticity of the apparitions and was a devotee of Our Lady of Fatima. We have already seen how in 1929 he had given an unofficial approval to the apparitions by distributing holy cards of Our Lady of Fatima to the seminarians of the Portuguese College of Rome. That was before the official recognition by the Bishop of Leiria, which was done in a pastoral letter in 1930.

What is certain is that Pope Pius XI, who reigned from 1922 to 1939, was supposed to make the requested consecration. This can be understood from the very words of Our Lady at the July 13 apparition, enunciating the reasons why she would come and ask for the consecration, as well as the spreading of the Communion of Reparation on the five First Saturdays. It seems the case to repeat them here:

> You have seen hell, where the souls of poor sinners go; in order to save them, God wants to establish devotion to My Immaculate Heart in the world. If they do what I tell you, many souls will be saved and there will be peace. The war will come to an end. But if they do not stop offending God, in the reign of Pius XI a worse war will begin. When you see a night illuminated by an unknown light, know that it is the great

sign that God gives you that He will punish the world for its crimes, by means of war, hunger and persecutions against the Church and the Holy Father.

To prevent it, I will come to ask for the consecration of Russia to My Immaculate Heart and the Communion of Reparation on the First Saturdays. If my requests are fulfilled, Russia will convert and there will be peace; if not, she will spread her errors throughout the world, promoting wars and persecutions of the Church. The good will be martyred, the Holy Father will have much to suffer and many nations will be annihilated. Finally, My Immaculate Heart will triumph. The Holy Father will consecrate Russia to me, she will convert and the world will be given some time of peace.

So we see that Our Lady indicated a general means for the salvation of souls, which is devotion to her Immaculate Heart: "In order to save them, God wants to establish devotion to my Immaculate Heart in the world."

Then she indicated, within this general means, that is, devotion to the Immaculate Heart of Mary, some specific means to obtain certain ends, namely the conversion of Russia, to avoid the war and all its consequences, including the dissemination of the "errors of Russia," persecutions of the Church and the Holy Father, the martyrdom of the good, the annihilation of many nations.

The specific means indicated were the consecration of Russia to the Immaculate Heart of Mary and the Communion of Reparation of the five First Saturdays. Indeed, soon after speaking about the new war that would break out at the time of Pius XI if her requests were not heeded, i.e., the Second World War, and the dissemination of the errors of Russia, and so forth, the Most Holy Virgin says, "To prevent it, I will come to ask for the consecration of Russia to My Immaculate Heart and the Communion of Reparation on the First Saturdays."

It is quite obvious that in the phrase, "to prevent it,"[1] the pronoun "it" refers to what had been mentioned earlier: the war and all its consequences that would ensue if the request were not heeded.

Therefore, it is entirely clear that the consecration of Russia to the Immaculate Heart of Mary was the means to avoid the Second World War and the brutal spread of Communism that followed it. So the consecration had to be done before the world conflict broke out; for if one must do *A* to prevent *B* from happening, one must do *A* before *B* happens.

Thus, for the consecration of Russia to have the effect desired by the Blessed Mother, it should have been made in the time span between 1929, the date it was requested, and 1939, the beginning of the Second World War. Now then, that period coincides with Pope Pius XI's pontificate, who was elected on February 6, 1922 and died on February 10, 1939.

The Consecration Should Have Been Made as Soon as It Was Asked

Now then, as we have seen above, in 1938 there was already a state of war. In fact, many historians consider the *Anschluss*, the annexation of Austria and its occupation by German troops on March 12, 1938, as part of World War II. Likewise, in the Munich Accord of September 1938, Germany obtained from France and Great Britain their *placet* to the annexation of the Sudetenland.

So, it would seem that in order to obtain the desired effects, the consecration of Russia to the Immaculate Heart of Mary

---

1. In the original: "[N]*o reinado de Pio XI começará outra guerra. .... Para **a** impedir, virei pedir a consagração da Russia....*" Now then, in Portuguese the demonstrative pronoun "***a***" is feminine and singular, and therefore it is replacing a feminine singular noun, that is, ***guerra*** "war."

should have been made before 1938. More likely, however, it should have been made in the beginning of the 1930s to avoid the great Communist advance that took place in that decade, the tragedy in Spain, as well as to stop Nazi Germany's quest for expansion that would lead to world wide conflagration.

Everything indicates, therefore, that the appropriate time for the consecration was precisely the moment when it was requested: around 1929–1930, perhaps even in 1935, before the Spanish Civil War. In any case, that consecration could never be done after World War II had begun, at least as a condition to avoid it, as had been promised at Fatima.

A Documented Confirmation

In many supernatural manifestations to Sister Lucia, Our Lord and Our Lady complained that the consecration had not been done and said that when it was done it would already be too late. In a letter of January 21, 1935, Sister Lucia writes Father Gonçalves, "As for Russia, it seems to me that Our Lord will be very pleased with your work for the Holy Father to fulfill His desires. Some three years ago Our Lord was very unhappy because his request was not fulfilled. . . . "

In another letter to the same priest, on May 18, 1936:

> As for the other question: If it would be well to insist in order to obtain the consecration of Russia. I answer almost the same as I have the other times. I am sorry it has not yet been done . . . I have spoken intimately with Our Lord about the matter, and just recently I asked Him why would He not convert Russia without His Holiness having made this consecration [He answered], "Because I want my whole Church to recognize this consecration as a triumph of the Immaculate Heart of Mary, to spread devotion to her and establish devotion to her Immaculate Heart in

The Consecrations

Undoubtedly, the chastisement predicted in case Russia was not consecrated to the Immaculate Heart of Mary has not ended. The consecrations carried out afterwards were certainly pleasing to God but, as the historical events clearly show, they no longer had the power to forestall the chastisement.

Here are the consecrations:

Pope Pius XII: On October 31, 1942, consecrated the Church and the human race to the Immaculate Heart of Mary, and on July 7, 1952, he consecrated the Russians to the Immaculate Heart of Mary.

Pope Paul VI: On November 21, 1964, confided the human race to the Immaculate Heart of Mary.

Pope John Paul II made two consecrations of the world to the Immaculate Heart of Mary: in Fatima on May 13, 1982; and in Rome on March 25, 1984.

Pope Benedict XVI on May 13, 2007 invoking Our Lady of Fatima on the ninetieth anniversary of the apparitions, stated, "In a special way we entrust to Mary those peoples and nations that are in particular need, confident that she will not fail to heed the prayers we make to her with filial devotion."

addition to the one to my Divine Heart."

Sister Lucia insists that the pope would not believe her words if God himself did not change his heart. To which Our Lord answers, "The Holy Father! Pray, pray much for the Holy Father. **He will do it, but it will be too late!** However, the Immaculate Heart of Mary will save Russia. It has been entrusted to Her."

Here Our Lady refers to the conversion of Russia after the

triumph of the Immaculate Heart of Mary, that is, after the trials of the chastisement, as stated in the Message of July 1917:

> "[Russia] will spread her errors throughout the world, promoting wars and persecutions of the Church, the good will be martyred, the Holy Father will have much to suffer and many nations will be annihilated: Finally, my Immaculate Heart will triumph. The Holy Father will consecrate Russia to me, which will convert and the world will be given some time of peace."

On another occasion, Our Lord communicated to Sister Lucia:

> "They did not want to fulfill my request. Like the king of France, **they will repent and will do it but it will be too late. Russia will already have scattered her errors throughout the world, provoking wars and persecutions of the Church**: The Holy Father will have much to suffer."[2]

In October 1940, when Sister Lucia wrote to Pope Pius XII proposing that the consecration of the world be made with a special mention of Russia, she no longer says that the consecration can avoid the chastisement but only that it can "abbreviate the days of tribulation with which [God] has determined to punish the nations for their crimes through war, hunger and many persecutions of the Church and of Your Holiness."

---

2. This is an allusion to the promise Our Lord made to Louis XIV through Saint Margaret Mary Alacoque. Our Lord promised to grant the king a life of grace and eternal glory, as well as victory over his enemies, if he would consecrate himself to the Sacred Heart, let it reign in his palace, paint it on his banners, and have it engraved on his coat of arms. As of 1792, after Louis XVI had been imprisoned in the Tower of the Temple, this request had still not been heeded. This king then made the vow to consecrate himself, his family, and his kingdom to the Sacred Heart of Jesus if he regained his freedom, the crown, and royal power. It was too late: the king left prison only for his execution.

CHAPTER 15
The "Errors of Russia"

"Russia . . . will spread its errors throughout the world, promoting wars and persecutions of the Church. . . . "

What were the errors that the Virgin predicted Russia would spread? It is Communism, a totalitarian sociopolitical and economic regime inspired by an atheistic and egalitarian doctrine opposed not only to the idea of Christian civilization but to the natural law as well.

Vladimir Lenin addressing the crown

The Communist Ideology

However, when speaking about the "errors of Russia," the Mother of God does more than just refer to a despotic and cruel socioeconomic regime created by an ideology. She refers directly to that ideology, the philosophical principles that sustain it, which became widespread in a broad but subtle manner: the Communist doctrine.

In his Encyclical *Divini Redemptoris*, of March 19, 1937, Pope Pius XI underlines the satanic character of Communism and its desire to destroy Christian civilization:

> We wish to expose once more in a brief synthesis the principles of atheistic Communism as they are manifested chiefly in bolshevism. We wish also to indicate its method of action and to contrast with its false principles the clear doctrine of the Church, in order to inculcate anew and with greater insistence the means by which Christian civilization, the true *civitas humana*, can be saved from the satanic

scourge, and not merely saved, but better developed for the well-being of human society.

Here is a summary of the Communist doctrine according to that Encyclical:

1. *Evolutionist materialism*—Communist doctrine is founded on the principles of the so-called dialectic materialism taught by Karl Marx. This doctrine proclaims the existence of only one universal reality formed by blind and hidden forces, which through natural evolution is transformed into plants, animals and men. By the same token, they claim, human society is nothing but an appearance or form of matter, which gradually evolves and, through an inexorable need and a perpetual conflict of forces, tends to a final synthesis: a classless society.

2. *Atheism*—This system has no place for the very idea of God; there is no difference at all between spirit and matter, soul and body; the soul does not survive after death, nor is there any life after this one.

3. *Class struggle*—The Communists, insisting on dialectic materialism, maintain that men are able to hasten the conflict that will lead to the final synthesis. This is why they strive to promote class struggle by exacerbating antagonisms among social classes.

4. *Depriving man of his liberty and dignity*—Communism strips man of his liberty and deprives him of his dignity, removing all restraints designed to help him resist the impulses of blind instinct. According to Communist theory, man is nothing but a cog in a wheel, and therefore Communists deny man's natural rights attributing those rights to the collective.

5. *Absolute equality*—The Communists advocate absolute equality and reject all hierarchy and authority coming

from God, even that of parents, claiming that all authority and subordination are derived from society.

6. *Negation of the right of private property*—Communism denies man's right to ownership of natural goods or of the means of production; since the latter produce other goods, their owner will be in a position of domination over others. For this reason they claim that the right of private property must be totally eliminated.

7. *Rejection of the sacred character of human life and of the family*—Communist doctrine denies the sacred character of human life and claims that matrimony and the family are mere fruits of the capitalist system. It consequently denies the indissoluble bonds of marriage.

8. *Robbing parents of the right to educate their children*—Even more, children are taken away from their homes to be cared for by the collective, that is, the State. Parents are thus robbed of their natural right to educate their offspring, which the Communists see as an exclusive right of the community that can only be exercised in its name.

9. *Negation of the Law and perennial Morals*—According to this doctrine, morals and the juridical order stem from the economic system; as a consequence, they are transient and changeable earthly values.

10. *The utopian ideal of a classless society with the abolition of the State*—Once their dreamed-of utopian ideal of a classless society is attained, the State will lose its reason for being and will be dissolved. Nevertheless, as long as that golden age is not reached, Communists will employ government and the public authority as the most effective instrument to attain their goal.

"Such, Venerable Brethren," the pope concludes,

> is the new gospel which bolshevistic and atheistic communism offers the world as the glad tidings of deliverance and salvation! It is a system full of errors and sophisms. It is in opposition both to reason and to Divine Revelation. It subverts the social order, because it means the destruction of its foundations; because it ignores the true origin and purpose of the State; because it denies the rights, dignity and liberty of human personality.

What have been the fruits of this doctrine's dissemination?

Communist Regimes: Terror and Atrocities

The same year Our Lady appeared at Fatima, a band of professional Communist revolutionaries led by Vladimir Lenin and Leon Trotsky violently seized power in Russia with the complicity of "moderates" like socialist Alexander Kerensky.

Czar Nicholas II was forced to abdicate and was arrested with his wife, Empress Alexandra, and five children. They were all murdered.

A long era of terror and injustice descended upon all countries dominated by Communism.

Joseph Stalin, Soviet dictator from 1924 until his death in 1953, became the symbol of Communist cruelty. He was responsible for millions of deaths.[1]

Since peoples everywhere have rejected Communism, its fanatic promoters have resorted to fraud, tricks and violence to

---

1. About 20 million deaths are attributed to him, including over 14.5 million from hunger in the period 1932–1934 of the collectivization of agriculture, especially in Ukraine. At least one million people were executed for political transgressions. To these are added 9.5 million who were deported or locked up in labor camps, more than 5 million of whom never returned alive from the gulags. Others put the number of deportees at 28 million, of which 18 million were shipped to the gulags.

impose it. Dictatorship has been a means to maintain unwilling populations submissive to that unnatural and egalitarian system.

In Spain, after the fall of the monarchy in 1931, and especially during the Civil War (1936–1939), the Communists perpetrated unspeakable atrocities against the Church: eleven bishops, more than 6,000 priests, countless numbers of religious and laity were killed in the cruelest ways.

In China, cruelty went hand-in-hand with propaganda and indoctrination. Mao Zedong embodies the very model of Communist cynicism that deceives the naïve and credulous. In spite of his easygoing looks he was responsible for the extermination of millions of innocent people.

In 1950, Communist China, through the puppet government in North Korea, invaded South Korea. Representing the United Nations, American troops were sent to defend that country against the Communists in the Korean War (1950–1954).

In 1959, Communist guerrilla warfare led Fidel Castro to power; Cubans have been subjected to terror and misery ever since.

The Vietnam War was fought to prevent Vietnam from falling under Communism. Political influences, however, prevented the United States military forces from winning; a peace treaty was imposed and the country was abandoned to Communism.

Communism spread to neighboring Cambodia, where it displayed all its horror. A large part of the population was systematically massacred to erase any remaining vestige of social, economic or intellectual inequality.

Is Communism Dead?

After the fall of the Berlin Wall and the collapse of the Soviet Union, many thought that Communism was dead. Is Communism really dead?

Officially, Russia and its former European satellites have rid themselves of Communism. Nevertheless, the KGB, the political security police of the Communist regime, has been given a new name but remains in place. And many of the new Russian leaders, including Vladimir Putin, come from the cadres of the KGB.

One should also bear in mind that Communist regimes remain active in China, Cuba, Laos, North Korea and Vietnam under the one-party system. Furthermore, President Vladimir Voronin of Moldova is a member of the Moldovan Communist Party, though Moldova does not have a one-party system.

The decrepit tyrant, Fidel Castro, continues to oppress Cubans and to promote guerrilla warfare in Central and South America. The FARC Communist guerrillas and other organizations have drenched Colombia with blood for nearly a half-century; and Venezuelan demagogue, Hugo Chavez, is the most faithful disciple of Castro in the area and is increasingly turning his dictatorial regime into that of his mentor's on the unfortunate Caribbean island.

Moreover, Communist parties or their successors continue to be politically important in many European, African, Asian and Latin-American countries.

The Errors of Russia Are More Active Than Ever

Moreover, even if we ignore the Communist regimes and political parties, whatever their names may be, as well as the guerrillas and other revolutionary forces fighting to seize power, we see the whole world moving almost imperceptibly toward Communism through the application of Communist principles:

1. In schools, students are taught the doctrine of evolutionism as a scientific dogma.
2. The presence of monuments to the Ten Commandments

and the invocation of God are forbidden in classrooms and in public places.

3. A climate of "class struggle" permeates relationships between employers and employees, professors and students, parents and children and so on, as well as between rich and poor nations;

4. Today's massified society deprives man of his individuality; a real dictatorship of the media and of powerful lobbies imposes the adoption of "politically correct" behaviors and inhibits any reaction against unbridled permissiveness.

5. Forces imbued with an egalitarian metaphysics seek to eliminate any inequality, be it in the family, society or the Church.

6. The right of property is being progressively eliminated by an ever growing tax burden.

7. Laws equating homosexual unions with marriage and promoting abortion and euthanasia are approved everywhere.

8. The ever growing State interference in children's education ends up by depriving parents of the right of raising their children according to their own values.

9. Moral relativism in fashions, cinema and television is widespread.

Thus, one can say that the errors of Russia today are more widespread than ever.

CHAPTER 16
"If They Do Not Stop Offending God"

The Fatima message can be summed up in a vehement appeal for the world's conversion. The Blessed Mother presented the devotion to her Immaculate Heart as a means to obtain special graces for that conversion. This devotion was to be manifested in the Communion of Reparation of the First Saturdays and the consecration of Russia as Our Lady requested.

If that way of mercy were rejected, justice would be meted out with the succession of chastisements that the Mother of God enumerated to the little shepherds.

A Succession of Chastisements

Our Lady listed the following punishments "if [men] do not stop offending God":

"In the reign of Pius XI another worse [war] will begin;

"Russia . . . will spread its errors throughout the world;

"Promoting wars and persecutions of the Church;

"The good will be martyred;

"The Holy Father will have much to suffer;

"Many nations will be annihilated."

When, after this whole series of punishments, men finally turn to God and a conversion takes place, not just of individuals but of society as such; of nations, recognizing the social kingship of Our Lord Jesus Christ and the Reign of Mary, then her promise will be realized: "Finally, My Immaculate Heart will triumph. The Holy Father will consecrate Russia to me, it will convert and the world will be given some time of peace."

"Promoting Wars . . ."

It would be well to emphasize that Our Lady distinguishes between two types of war that would come as punishment:

the Second World War and the "wars" caused by the diffusion of the errors of Russia.

After the Fatima apparitions, in addition to the Second World War there were countless other wars, some clearly caused by Communists (such as in Korea and Vietnam, or the Chinese Civil War known as the "Nationalist-Communist Civil War" of 1927–1949, which culminated with the implantation of the Communist regime in China). The Communist factor was also at work in other wars such as the Spanish Civil War of 1936–1939 or the Greek Civil War of 1944–1945 and 1946–1949, in which the Communists were defeated; and in the colonial wars in Africa in the 1960s and 1970s. Furthermore, Communist guerrilla warfare spread on various continents, with guerrilla groups still very active in South America, Asia and Africa. Finally, have the "errors of Russia" not been favored by Islamic terrorism, which seeks to destroy what still remains of Christian civilization in the Western world? How else can one explain the ill-disguised sympathy of the international left toward Islamic terrorists?

"Persecutions of the Church . . ."

The Church has been suffering two types of persecution: bloody persecution in some countries, especially in Muslim and Communist ones, and persecution by means of laws and restrictions on the preaching of Church doctrine, particularly in reference to morals, and through a continuing wave of blasphemies and insults.

"The Good Will Be Martyred . . ."

Note that Our Lady said that the "good" will be martyred. This appears to indicate that a time will come when it will suffice for anyone to want to be good, that is, faithful to the observance of the Ten Commandments or simply of the Natural

Law, even without taking any militant or challenging stance, to become a victim of those who propagate or uphold the "errors of Russia."

As a matter of fact, the homosexual movement has acquired such power these days in the United States and in countless other countries where "hate crime" laws have been approved, that one can ask whether that persecution is not already quite advanced. Indeed, it is becoming increasingly difficult for anyone to live in a way consistent with right principles and reject unnatural sexual practices without being subject to retaliation.

"The Holy Father Will Have Much to Suffer . . ."

This is the consequence of the persecution against the Church and the good. The Church is not only the custodian of Divine Revelation, which the Church explains with authority, but is also the guardian of Natural Law. The Church cannot, in any case, accept as legitimate acts such as free love and homosexual practice that are aberrant to nature because these are contrary to their natural end.

Sooner or later, the scorn that the media has been pouring on Catholics and the Church will turn against the Holy Father himself, as the attack on Pope John Paul II on May 13, 1981, and the prophecies of Jacinta lead us to suppose.

"Many Nations Will Be Annihilated . . ."

This statement has a political meaning, signifying that many nations will lose their sovereignty and cease to exist as independent nations; a physical, material meaning, as a result of cataclysms of great magnitude such as a giant tsunami that destroys a whole coastal area; or a succession of earthquakes, seaquakes and fires; or still, a nuclear hecatomb that sweeps entire nations, leaving them totally depopulated, destroyed, "annihilated"; and a psychological and cultural meaning: as

"Such as I Love, I Rebuke and Chastise"

Some could object to this possibility of chastisement with the idea that God, being Goodness itself, never punishes men.

Actually, since God is the absolute perfect being, and the cause of all perfection, He must have in Himself all possible perfections. Thus, He is not only infinitely good and merciful, but also infinitely just. As the Psalmist so aptly says, "Mercy and truth have met each other: justice and peace have kissed" (Psalm 84:11).

In the book of the Apocalypse, God says, "Such as I love, I rebuke and chastise. Be zealous therefore, and do penance. Behold, I stand at the gate, and knock" (Apocalypse 3:19–20).

Therefore, while God reserves definitive reward or punishment for the next life, as seen in the parable of the wheat and the chaff (Matt. 13:24–30), He also chastises on this earth. This truth is formally found in Revelation. Some examples are: the plagues of Egypt (Exodus, chapters 7–8); the Flood (Genesis, chapters 6–8); the destruction of Sodom and Gomorrah (Genesis, chapter 19); and the destruction of Jerusalem (Matt. 24:1–2).

occurred, for example, with the Roman Empire of the West as a consequence of the barbarian invasions.

Instead of Conversion, a Challenge to God

Unfortunately, instead of heeding the merciful appeals of Our Lady at Fatima, men appear to have chosen the way of perdition, except for a considerable minority of people who take the Blessed Mother's words seriously and that, thanks be to God, has been growing steadily over the years.

Men have not only chosen the way of sin but have picked forms of sin that do not stem from weakness, albeit culpable, but constitute a type of sin in which the sinner takes pride, despises and persecutes virtue and, even worse, challenges God.

Abortion becomes the official law of the land, unions against nature are placed on equal footing with marriage, euthanasia is adopted, people wear clothes that emphasize the most intimate parts of the human body, nudism or semi-nudism spreads on the beaches and elsewhere—all this is a proclamation of man's rejection of the Law of God.

Even worse, challenging God's wrath, strident parades and demonstrations are held on the national and international levels to display "pride" for practices against nature, picking for this end the more symbolic places like Rome, the capital of Christianity, in the Holy Jubilee Year of 2000; and in 2006, Jerusalem, the city sanctified by the passion and death of Our Lord Jesus Christ.

Can God remain insensitive to such grievous challenges?

CONCLUSION
"Finally, My Immaculate Heart Will Triumph!"

While some of the chastisements announced at Fatima have already been fulfilled, others are still to come. Yet, however painful and gloomy the outlook may be, we should not become discouraged, as we are also animated by the confidence of victory.

Confidence in Our Lady

Saint Thomas explains that "confidence" (*fiducia*) takes its name from "faith" (*fides*). It is a hope fortified by the faith that we have in someone's help. That faith will be all the greater the more powerful that person is and the greater the friendship, love and compassion that person has for us.

When that person is the Mother of God and our Mother, we have the very best reason in the world to confide in her, since she is united with God totally and loves us enormously. Furthermore, the Blessed Mother announced that, after the chastisements that would come as a consequence of the rejection of her requests and the lack of conversion of mankind, her Immaculate Heart would triumph.

The certainty of the triumph of the Immaculate Heart of Mary, of the conversion of Russia, and of the time of peace that will come after the succession of punishments in which we are still immersed, should encourage us in the highest degree and inspire us to do our part in the struggle for that promised triumph.

A Necessary Collaboration

As Professor Plinio Corrêa de Oliveira, the founder of the Brazilian TFP and a great apostle of Fatima, emphasized, there is nothing in the message given to the little shepherds that would be contrary to the idea of our participating in the struggle for the triumph of the Immaculate Heart of Mary.

It is in the plans of Divine Providence that men should participate in the struggle for historical transformations and serve as instruments, though imperfect, for the action of divine grace.

The Appeal Is Also Addressed to Us

The appeal for prayer and penance made to the little shepherds nearly a century ago still resounds today, because, through them, it is equally addressed to us.

The struggle can be an excellent form of prayer and penance, when engaged in for the love of God.

To oppose today's neopagan ambience; combat the errors, at times subtle, that are spread by every means; and to face the risk of being disliked for not following fashions, both in dressing and thinking, is often much more difficult than fasting or spending a night in prayer.

By the way, one thing does not exclude the other: To pray in public, thus combating human respect and proclaiming the Faith, is one of the most excellent forms of penance nowadays.

Yes, penance and prayer for the conversion of sinners is what the Blessed Mother is asking of us. However, she expects us to do even more: To combat the "errors of Russia" that continue to triumph right before our eyes destroying families, corrupting our youth, and blaspheming God.

Let us do our part, confiding in the fulfillment of her promise, "Finally, my Immaculate Heart will triumph!"

BIBLIOGRAPHY

There is a huge bibliography on Fatima. Here we list only the books we have actually consulted to write this brief study of the Fatima apparitions and the lives of the three seers, Lucia, Jacinta and Francisco. Obviously, the main source is the *Memórias da Irmã Lucia*, published by Father Luis Kondor, S.V.D.

Baker, G. Leslie. *The Finger of God is Here*, St. Paul Publications, Middle Green, 1961.

Barthas, Canon C., Da Fonseca, S.J., Father G. *Our Lady of Light*, The Bruce Publishing Company, Milwaukee, 1947.

Borelli, Antonio A., Spann, John R., Corrêa de Oliveira, Plinio. *Our Lady at Fatima: Prophecies of tragedy or hope for America and the world?*, The American Society for the Defense of Tradition, Family and Property, Spring Grove-PA, 1986.

De Marchi, I.M.C., Father John, The Immaculate Heart—*The True Story of Our Lady of Fatima*, Farrar, Straus and Young, New York, 1952.

Documentação Crítica de Fatima (Processo Canónico Diocesano—1922–1930), Santuário de Fatima, 1999.

Galamba De Oliveira, Father José. *Jacinta—The Flower of Fatima* (Rev. Humberto S. Medeiros and Rev. William F. Hill, translators), Catholic Book Publishing Co., New York, 1946.

Haffert, John M. *Meet the Witnesses*, The American Society For The Defense Of Tradition, Family and Property—TFP, Spring Grove, Penn. 2006.

Kondor, S.V.D, Father Luís (Ed.). *Memórias da Irmã Lucia*, Vol. I, 1ª.–4ª. Memórias, Compilação do Pe. Luís Kondor, S.V.D., Vice-Postulação, Fatima, Portugal, 7ª. Edição, Maio de 1997.

Kondor, S.V.D, Father Luís (Ed.). *Memórias da Irmã Lucia*, Vol. II, 5ª.–6ª. Memórias, Secretariado dos Pastorinhos, Fatima, Portugal, 1999.

Martins, S.J., Pe. António Maria (Ed.). Novos Documentos de Fatima, Livraria A.I., Porto, 1984.

Martins, S.J., Pe. Dr. António Maria (Ed.). *Memórias e Cartas da Irmã Lucia* (edição trilingue, português, francês e inglês), L.E., Porto, 1973.

McGlynn, O.P., Thomas. *Vision of Fatima*, Garden City Books, Garden City, N.Y., 1951.

Michel de la Sainte Trinité, Frère. *The Whole Truth About Fatima*, vols. I & II, Immaculate Heart Publications, Buffalo-Ontario, 1989.

Rengers, O.F.M.Cap., Christopher. *The Youngest Prophet— The Life of Jacinta Marto, Fatima Visionary*, Alba House, New York, 1986.

Rolim, Pe. Francisco. *Florinhas de Fatima*, Lisboa, 1944.

Walsh, William Thomas. *Our Lady of Fatima*, Image Books, New York, 1954.